Nobody's Perfect

You're special to God—in spite of yourself

Nobody's Perfect

by Terry Powell

This book is designed for your personal reading pleasure and profit. It is also designed for group study. A leader's guide, with visual aids (SonPower Multiuse Transparency Masters) is available from your local Christian bookstore or from the publisher.

VICTOR BOOKS

a division of SP Publications, Inc., Wheaton, Illinois
Offices also in Fullerton, California • Whitby, Ontario, Canada • London, England

Second printing, 1979

Bible quotations are from the following versions: (NASB) —*New American Standard Bible,* © 1960, 1962, 1963, 1968, 1971, 1972, 1973, by the Lockman Foundation, (PH)—*The New Testament in Modern English,* © J. B. Phillips 1958, The Macmillan Company, (LB)—*The Living Bible,* © Tyndale House Publishers, Wheaton, Illinois; (NIV)—*The New International Version: New Testament,* © 1973, The New York Bible Society International.

Passages from *Love is Now* by Peter E. Gillquist, © 1970, 1978 by Zondervan Publishing House. Used by permission.

Library of Congress Catalog Card Number: 78-65556
ISBN: 0-88207-577-2

VICTOR BOOKS
A division of SP Publications, Inc.
P.O. Box 1825 ● Wheaton, Ill. 60187

Dedicated to my dad,
George Powell,
of Ellenboro, North Carolina

His love for Jesus and his solid
reputation as a Christian made
me proud to call him "Dad."

Contents

WORLD'S
GREATEST
SKATEBOARDER

1

Being a Successful Failure

"I should've known better than to let a freshman pitch!" bellowed the coach, as I slouched dejectedly on the bench after the game. His remark made me cringe, embarrassing me more than the opposing team's hitting streak.

I had blown my first starting assignment as a high school pitcher. The only times my "fast" ball picked up speed were when the other team slapped line drives. I figured the coach would assign me to permanent bullpen duty.

At the time, baseball was the most important thing in my life. That's why I couldn't shrug off the poor performance with an easy, "I'll get 'em next time!" It hurt to fail. I secretly wished the game had been rained out.

Failure: A Common Denominator

Failing can be gut-ripping. Society expects us to be successful. Whether we succeed often determines how we feel about ourselves. But let's face it: The road to success is cratered with hidden chuckholes. Believe it or not, no one succeeds all the time. Falling short of what God, parents, and friends expect of us is one of the ugly experiences of life.

Several high school students told me about their experiences with failure. Brad mentioned bombing out in an English literature course. "Reading isn't my thing, you know. I've dreaded that class ever since I flunked the first exam. Oh, I'll get by with a D, but to my folks, that's failing. To them, anything less than a B+ is bad news."

Kay, a new Christian, said, "I told my best friend why I believe in Jesus, but she didn't buy it. She asked a lot of questions about God and the Bible that I couldn't answer. I was so embarrassed! I don't think I'll ever get up enough nerve to mention Jesus again!"

A poor excuse for a Christian—that's how Amy felt. "I know it's wrong, but I keep going out with guys who aren't Christians. I'm almost afraid to pray to God now, knowing I've let Him down."

Being the only junior in a sophomore-filled Driver Ed class made Steve self-conscious. When he flunked the drivers test, he wanted to crawl under the floor mat.

Anna is sure something is terribly wrong with her. After all, she had only two dates all last year. And they weren't very exciting at that.

Why do feelings of failure hang on almost everyone like vicious blood-sucking leeches? What is the basic difference between those who succeed and those who fail? How should faith in Jesus affect the way we react to failure? How can God use our goofs to help us grow spiritually? In God's Word we find responses to these questions—not with mystical grin-and-bear-it explanations, but through stories of men and women who loved, laughed, and cried as we do. People who, like you and me, knew what it was like to fall short.

Let's stop pretending Bible personalities were superpeople. Those who eventually achieved a lot for God sometimes experienced the one step-forward-and-two-steps-backward routine too. For instance, consider John Mark.

Portrait of a Failure

John Mark's background wasn't one you'd find described in the *Who's Who* in Jerusalem, his hometown. He didn't walk on water, nor did people flock to him wanting the great mysteries of life revealed. He was probably just an average, run-of-the-mill Jewish kid.

"John" means "God is gracious" and points to his Jewish heritage. But most folks called him by his Roman name, Mark.

His mother's name was Mary. Don't confuse her with other Marys of the New Testament: the mother of Jesus, the mother of James, or Mary Magdalene.

Though his family was rather wealthy, Mark still had problems. His father probably died while Mark was young. Mark may well have been physically handicapped, biblical authorities think. Somebody gave him a nickname meaning "stump-fingered."

During Paul's first missionary journey, Mark deserted Paul and his cousin Barnabas. In A.D. 47, the church in Antioch sent Paul and Barnabas to preach in faraway places. They took Mark with them. Mark probably managed business details and assisted in counseling new converts. But in Perga, Turkey, Mark suddenly quit and took the first boat back home to Jerusalem (Acts 13:13).

Why did Mark quit? The first leg of the journey had taken them to Cyprus, which was familiar to him. But when he reached Perga, Mark faced the area's bandits and natural hazards. Perhaps Mark's knees got a little shaky as he considered the real and imaginary dangers of a trip across the rugged Tarsus mountains through almost trackless forest. Paul and Barnabas didn't plan on Mark's quick exit. Paul resented what he considered to be Mark's desertion in a crisis (Acts 15:38).

Mark's cowardice drove a steel wedge between two close friends. From what we read in Acts 15:36-41, we can imagine a conversation between Paul and Barnabas:

BARNABAS: Yeah, I really think we ought to go back where we preached to keep the people from going back to their old ways, as you said. But don't you think we need a little help?

PAUL: Who'd you have in mind?

BARNABAS: Well, maybe, I was sort of thinking of Mark.

PAUL: Mark!

BARNABAS: Why not?

PAUL: You gotta be kidding! He chickened out on us back in Perga. The trip'll be hard enough without having to baby-sit him.

BARNABAS: Aw, give him another chance.

PAUL: No! He's not going—and that's final! I don't care if he *is* your cousin.

So Paul and Barnabas split. Instead of Barnabas, Paul took Silas to Syria and Cilicia, while Barnabas and Mark sailed to Cyprus.

It's interesting to note that Paul didn't consider Mark worth replacing. Silas replaced Barnabas. Paul didn't chose a successor to Mark. Paul and Barnabas parted in anger. As far as we know, they never met again (Acts 15:39).

The breach was later healed, for Paul spoke kindly of Barnabas in his letters (1 Corinthians 9:6 and Galatians 2:9). But they never again worked as a team.

How do you think Mark felt when friends asked about his sudden return from the mission field? When he found out what Paul had said about him? He felt bad, of course. He thought he was inferior. Guilty. If anyone ever had reason to feel sorry for himself, to say, "I'm not cut out to serve Jesus," it was Mark.

But he didn't resign himself to being a second-class citizen in God's kingdom. And that's why the rest of his story is so interesting.

The Rest of the Story

Barnabas wasn't willing just to forget about Mark. So he took him along to Cyprus. The Bible doesn't give details of Mark's years immediately following his quick exit in Antioch. But we know God later used this unlikely candidate to achieve great results.

Mark helped Paul in Rome. Time had changed Paul's opinion of Mark. In A.D. 67, while serving with Mark in Asia Minor, Timothy received a letter from Paul. Paul told Timothy, "Pick up Mark and bring him with you, for he is useful to me for service" (2 Timothy 4:11, NASB.) Paul specifically encouraged the Colossians to welcome Mark when he visited, because Paul's former negative opinion of Mark had probably reached the ears of many Christians over a wide area.

What a contrast! Formerly the butt of Paul's anger; later, the object of Paul's praise. Once branded a quitter; later called a useful worker in God's kingdom.

Mark's written account of Jesus' ministry, the Gospel according to Mark, was his greatest contribution to Christianity. The Holy Spirit used Peter to furnish Mark with the details of his narrative.

It's impossible to overestimate the importance of Mark's Gospel. It was probably the first Gospel, written between A.D. 50 and 55. For the first time, persons who weren't within earshot of evangelists such as Peter and Paul could receive the message of Jesus. The Holy Spirit led Matthew and Luke to reproduce parts of Mark's work in their volumes about Jesus. For centuries, Mark's Gospel has been the first part of Scripture translated into new languages after primitive tribes have been reached.

According to a church historian named Eusebius, Mark established churches in Alexandria. He succeeded at the church-planting mission he had run away from as a young man!

It's exciting to see what God could do with a fatherless, possibly even deformed, chicken-hearted kid! To stay down, to brood over our mistakes, is our natural tendency. What motivated Mark to get up and try again? What did he learn that can make a difference for 20th-century failures?

Jesus Gives Us a Second Chance (and Third and Fourth . . .)

Mark's change of mind shows the forgiveness of Jesus Christ. Barnabas forgave Mark. He saw Mark's potential rather than his failure. He gave Mark a fresh chance. Barnabas' love for Mark is a reflection of Jesus' love for us.

Society labels us failures if we don't measure up to its standards. And we compare ourselves with others to see if we've made it. But Jesus doesn't withdraw His love from us when we make mistakes. He doesn't parcel out His love on the basis of looks, grades, athletic success, or economic status. There are two types of failure. Spiritual failure refers to sin or disobedience to biblical commands. Natural failure refers to shortcomings, or lack of certain abilities, which keep us from reaching some personal goal or social standard. When failures drag us down and sin isn't the cause, it's usually because our definition of success is wrong. Christianity is good news because it says our worth—and our acceptability before God—isn't based on our own performance.

God's standard is perfection. No one measures up to it. We're all sons and daughters of Adam. From him we inherited selfishness and rebellion. So by nature, we're all failures! But God visited this planet in the form of Jesus Christ. Jesus paid the penalty for our errors. When we agree that He assumed the punishment we deserve and receive Him as Saviour, we stand forgiven of all sins—past, present, and future.

Have you seen a computer with a TV-type screen being operated? When the programmer makes an error, he presses the "cancel" button. That automatically eliminates all information from the screen. The programmer begins his calculations again without trying to sort out previous mistakes. There's not even a record of the mistake—it's lost forever! That's what happens to our sins when God forgives us (Hebrews 10:17). Consequences sometimes remain, but the sin is gone (Romans 8:1).

In God's eyes, how we respond to Jesus is the difference between success and failure. If we're already Christians, we can relax in what Jesus' sacrifice accomplished for us. It's easy to question our status with God after failing Him. But when we think we're second-class Christians, we're actually questioning Jesus' own acceptability before God the Father!

Grasping this truth can keep us from trying to snow God. There's no need to shy away from Him when we mess up. We can give our failures to the One who can do something about them. This realization of Jesus' forgiveness helped Mark bounce back.

How We Respond to Failure Is the Greatest Test of Our Faith in Christ

We have limited natural abilities. We won't be sinless till we're with Jesus. Mark's life teaches us to accept our weaknesses as we develop our areas of strength. Every Christian can serve God (1 Peter 4:10).

We can either withdraw or try again. We can either feel guilty or accept forgiveness. When we fail, it's easy to concentrate too much on our problems and mistakes.

In *The Screwtape Letters*, C. S. Lewis vividly describes Satan's strategy: He gets Christians to become preoccupied with their failures; from then on, his battle is won.

A Bible teacher assigned his students an outreach project in a tough area of town. One student came up to the teacher and whispered, "I have laryngitis. I—I can't talk. Can I be excused from this project?"

"You haven't lost your voice," replied the teacher abruptly. "You're chicken!"

"I'm not!" answered the student.

"Listen," the teacher continued. "I'm a coward too. The only difference between you and me is this: I've decided to relate my fear to Somebody who isn't afraid, and you've decided to worship your fear!"

Mark was chicken. Yet he had faith in what Jesus could do with him. God enjoys getting hold of losers. "Consider your calling, brethren, that there are not many wise according to the flesh, not many mighty, not many noble; but God has chosen the foolish things of the world to shame the wise, and God has chosen the weak things of the world to shame the things which are strong, and the base things of the world and the despised . . . the things that are not . . . that no man should boast before God" (1 Corinthians 1:26-29, NASB).

Mark's transformation offers hope for needed changes in our lives. God is in the construction business. Observing His carpentry work on Mark should convince us that He can rebuild our minds, help us overcome bad habits, and cause us to love persons we dislike.

Failure, Then Success

The key to success is a growing faith in Jesus. If personal limitations and sin cause us to rely more on Him than on ourselves, then failure becomes a stepping-stone to success!

God's will for us isn't lost because we fail. Our past mistakes don't limit God's power. What Christ can do for us in the future is more important than the mistakes we've made in the past.

Mark didn't blow it for eternity because he chickened out once. The past can't be changed, but our response to it can. In his letter to the Philippians (3:4-7), Paul lists the false goals that dominated his life as a Pharisee. He mentions his former persecution of Christians. But once he discovered the truth about Jesus, he didn't sit around feeling miserable about all the time he had wasted. Like Mark, he knew God had a plan for people despite their failure.

Paul writes, "One thing I do: Forgetting what lies behind and reaching forward to what lies ahead, I press on toward the goal for the prize of the upward call of God in Christ Jesus!" (Philippians 3:13-14, NASB).

What Paul wrote for the Philippians can be true for you: "For I am confident of this very thing, that He who began a good work in you will perfect it until the day of Christ Jesus" (Philippians 1:6, NASB).

If you feel like a failure, take heart! Get excited about what God wants to accomplish through you, knowing what He did through John Mark.

2

How Sorry Can You Get?

Todd, a high school junior, was the most popular guy in his church youth group. His sense of humor and beaming personality drew you to him. He sang in a quartet and played guitar for the youth choir. Todd's youth director often chose him to help visiting teens who expressed an interest in knowing Christ.

Then one mistake changed Todd's life.

It happened late one Sunday evening. He had sex with his girlfriend. Afterward, Todd felt so guilty that he refused to go to church and face his friends. A few months later, he dropped out of high school.

One of his Christian friends reminded Todd of Jesus' forgiveness. "I just can't believe God can forget what I did that easily!" Todd replied. He found it hard to live with himself. He was afraid that God's forgiveness was too good to be true.

We've all done things we're ashamed of. Guilt

is a problem a lot of us have, a nagging awareness that we've blown it and let God down. Ironically, guilt haunts Christians more than it does unbelievers. We often think we don't measure up.

Several Ways to Handle Guilt

Some people try to suppress guilt by working harder, busily witnessing, teaching, or singing in a choir. Subconsciously, they hope to win a pat on the head from God.

It's hard to believe some of the things people do in order to feel forgiven. A missionary from South America told me about a group of idol-worshipers who crawl on their knees for miles toward a sacred temple. When they reach the temple steps, they slowly and painfully climb the steps—on their bare knees—till they reach the idol in the temple. The ritual takes days to complete, and their knees are torn and bleeding by the time it's over. That's their way of trying to please their god.

We wouldn't stoop to skinning our knees. But when we try to cover up guilt with good works, we're trying to fool God the same way.

Other people handle guilt by blaming the next guy or circumstances. ("It just happened all by itself.") They won't claim responsibility for their actions. They say unjust acts by those around them made them do what they did.

Another favorite way of handling guilt is to tame your conscience, convincing yourself that what you did wasn't wrong after all. Adolph Eichmann, a Nazi who helped murder 6 million

Jews a few decades ago, didn't feel guilty. He said he'd jump into his grave with glee, believing he hadn't done anything wrong.

In his book *I Never Promised You a Disneyland,* Jay Kesler calls yet another way of handling guilt the "Harper Valley PTA" mentality. Kesler says, " 'Harper Valley PTA' was a song quite a few years ago where a lady who's being put down by PTA members goes to their meeting and tells them how bad *they* are. The implication is, 'I'm better than you, because we're all bad, but I don't pretend to be better than what I am. At least I'm honest.' Well, being honest doesn't count for much if you're just honest about being bad. You're still bad."

Most people, though, handle guilt Todd's way. They know they blew it and they're willing to admit it. That sounds noble. Certainly it's better to be weighed down with grief than to refuse to admit wrongdoing. Yet just being sorry isn't enough. Todd felt sorry, but his life was still a mess.

Why is feeling sorry for sins we've comitted an imcomplete answer to guilt? What's the difference between worldly sorrow, like Todd felt, and godly sorrow that leads to a lasting positive change?

For answers, let's look at one of the most despised characters in the Bible: Judas Iscariot. We may see ourselves in the tragic way he handled guilt. We have to avoid his pattern of thought before we can experience refreshing, without-a-doubt assurance of God's forgiveness.

Unpopular Name

How many guys in your school or at work go by the name "Judas"?

Probably none. But for centuries, it was a common name among Jews. The Bible mentions a least nine different persons by that name. But ever since Judas Iscariot betrayed Jesus for 30 pieces of silver, the name has meant "traitor."

We know nothing about Judas' early life. He's first mentioned in Jesus' choosing of the Twelve Disciples. Judas at first really wanted to help Jesus set up a new kingdom. He didn't plan from the start to turn his back on Jesus.

Judas began losing faith in Jesus during the final months of His ministry. He couldn't digest all Jesus' talk about dying on a cross. He figured that Jesus' mission was political, that He'd use His supernatural power to help Israel overthrow the Roman Empire. When it became clear that Jesus was more concerned about ruling men's hearts than ruling their countries, Judas felt frustrated. Seeds of disillusionment began growing in his heart.

Judas Acts

The first evidence of Judas' changing attitude came a few days before the crucifixion, at a dinner in Bethany. Friends had planned a dinner in Jesus' honor. Mary, Lazarus' sister, showed her love for Jesus by rubbing His feet with perfume. What she used was more expensive than a bottle of the costliest Chanel No. 5. The average person would have had to work for a year to earn enough money to buy that bottle of imported aroma.

That seemingly senseless act burned Judas up. He said they could have sold the perfume and given the money to the poor. (Judas was in charge of the disciples' treasury.) But John indicates it was greed—not concern for the poor—that prompted Judas' outburst. Had the perfume been sold, the cash would have become available to Judas. (John says Judas often dipped into the disciples' fund for his own use.) Since Judas hadn't been greedy from the beginning, some authorities think that perhaps his discouragement over the nature of Jesus' mission made him more vulnerable to temptation.

When Judas criticized Mary, Jesus scolded him. That's about when he began bargaining with Jewish religious leaders for money to betray Him. Days later, during Jesus' final meal with the disciples, Judas excused himself and closed the deal. Later that evening, he led the arresting party to the garden of Gethsemane. There he identified Jesus for the mob by embracing and kissing Him.

Some think Judas never wanted Jesus to die, that he just tried to force Jesus to flex supernatural muscles and start an armed revolt. But since death was part of God's plan for Him, Jesus went along with the mob. However, the Bible indicates that Satan's direct influence, along with disillusionment over Jesus' mission and greed, caused Judas' actions.

When the authorities sentenced Jesus to death, Judas felt guilty. He couldn't reconcile what he'd done with Jesus' teaching about love and loyalty. That an innocent man was going to die pricked his conscience. He tried to undo things by giving back the 30 pieces of silver, but the Jewish leaders sneered and refused the money. Then he used a different approach to prove how sorry he felt. He killed himself.

Sorry—God's Way

The same evening, another disciple also went through a guilt crisis. Peter had claimed that he'd never desert Jesus. But while outside the building where Jesus was standing trial, he got scared. A girl asked him if he were one of Jesus' followers. Peter swore he wasn't. Two more times that evening he denied knowing anything about Jesus. He remembered that Jesus had predicted his denials, and he came unglued. Peter ran out and cried.

Like Judas, Peter had blown it with God, and felt sorry. Later, though, Peter served as a dynamic church leader whose sermons God used to convert thousands to Christianity. Why did Judas' life end so abruptly, when Peter enjoyed 30 or more extra years as a successful leader?

The difference between Peter and Judas, according to Jay Kesler, was "in the object of the sorrow. The remorseful man puts all the blame on himself, and keeps it there. He wants it to weigh him down so he and everyone else will know he's sorry. That's what Judas did.

"But the repentant man—the one who's sorry in God's way—puts the guilt and the pain on the cross by trusting Jesus' forgiveness. He leaves it there, and goes on following Jesus. That's what Peter did" (*I Never Promised You a Disneyland*).

Kesler also tells a story about a man riding down the road on a donkey while he carried a 200-pound sack of wheat on his shoulders. Somebody spotted him and asked, "Why don't you take the weight off your shoulders and put it on the donkey?" The rider replied, "You don't think I'm going to ask the donkey to carry all that weight, do you?"

We're like the man with the wheat when we pray about our sins, but still mope around carrying the emotional burden of all the things we're sorry for. We don't trust God to forgive and forget. Instead we keep putting ourselves down and dousing ourselves in self-pity. Either we believe God is willing to forgive us, or we don't!

Putting the weight of sin where it belongs—on Jesus' back, not ours—is something we have to keep working on. He's willing to pick us up when we fall, and to help us grow so we won't fall quite so often.

Case Dismissed!

Jesus is more than just a beast of burden. The Bible calls Jesus our "Advocate" or "Defense Attorney."

I'm glad He exercises this role. Satan often tries to arouse guilt feelings in me for sins I've already prayed about. He wants me to feel sad instead of asking for forgiveness so I'll put the blame on myself instead of on Jesus.

When I feel guilty, I picture a courtroom in heaven. I'm the defendant. Jesus is my lawyer. God sits on the bench, and Satan is the prosecuting attorney. Satan has solid proof that I just broke God's law. He confidently presents his case: "OK, God, here's the Christian You said was blameless. See what he did! Are You going to let him get away with it?"

Then Jesus, my Counsel, steps before the bench. "Father, You and I agreed that My death on the cross included this sin just like all the others. I've already paid the penalty for it. Terry has trusted me as His Saviour, so the sin has been placed on My account. Why should he have to stand trail for a sin I've already paid for?"

Next I hear the rap of a gavel. God says, "Case dismissed!"

The Todds of this world, those who never accept Jesus' redeeming power, have given themselves a life sentence of misery without hope of parole. They're spending time for sins that Jesus has already been executed for. If they could only grasp that we have a God who gives fresh chances.

3
Impossible Obedience

Why Trust God?
Trust *You* with my life?
God, that's the same as saying,
"Here, it's Yours now."
I'm not sure I'm ready for that.
I'm afraid to say, "You take over, God."
It's risky.
What will happen to *my* plans?
I have my own ideas about
whom to date
where to go
how to spend my time and money
what to do after graduation.
I want to be sure
before I give my life away
that You won't spoil things for me.
God,
If I trust You with my life,
what will You do with it?

I wrote that poem years ago while struggling to come up with my concept of God. At the time, doing things God's way didn't seem like much fun. I wondered: *Is God a spoilsport who gets His kicks in saying no to fun and freedom?* Or has He mapped out a better plan for my life than I have? Oh, I'd have agreed with anyone who called Him a loving God. But my not being willing to trust Him—to let Him take control of my life—proved I wasn't really sure.

A researcher asked a cross section of churchgoing young people, "What is your impression of the Bible?" One fellow summed up the attitude of the majority: "It's like a nagging mother!" How we see God and His words in the Bible affects how we live. It's impossible to enjoy a relationship with someone whose words come across like those of a nagging parent.

Why is a negative view of God and His Word so often heard? How does our concept of God affect our response to Him? What truths can remove our fear of trusting and obeying? On which of the various motives for obedience does God put His stamp of approval? Where do we get the strength to obey those demands that appear impossible? What happens when we accept God's ways rather than yield to natural impulses?

We can find some answers to these questions by looking at one first-century Christian's life. Let's examine the story of Philip the evangelist, who was known for the way he obeyed God. Let's see what God has told us about obedience through Philip's life.

The Treasures of the King

When Elvis Presley died in 1977, he left behind a dazzling assortment of personal things.

In his famous Graceland mansion in Memphis, there were 17 paintings and portraits of Presley, 37 pistols and other firearms, 200 pairs of trousers, and 242 chairs, couches, and cushions. About 60 different pieces of nightwear, including elegant pajamas with matching night caps, crowded his bedside closet. From his bed, Elvis watched TV on either of two color screens installed in the ceiling. He owned eight cars and jeeps, ranging from a 1921 Stutz Bearcat to a 1976 Chevrolet pickup custom de luxe.

Of course, Elvis had more money than most of us. Even on a smaller scale, though, it's easy to get hung up on things that aren't important.

Philip didn't jump on this get-all-you-can-while-you-can-get-it bandwagon. Giving, not getting, marked his life-style. People, not status or material things, were the object of his investment. Telling about Christ, not himself, motivated his behavior.

Don't confuse Philip the evangelist with the disciple of Christ by the same name. The Gospels don't mention the evangelist. Because he was "of good reputation, full of the Spirit and of wisdom" (Acts 6:3, NASB), church leaders in Jerusalem gave Philip and six others the job of running a feeding program for widows. When Jews began persecuting the church, Philip ran from Jerusalem to Samaria. Without the aid of today's slick advance men to organize and publicize a crusade, he began preaching Christ to the Samaritans.

Philip astounded his listeners with miracles of healing and exorcism. People in droves deserted a man named Simon who had hoodwinked them with magical tricks, and turned to Christ. Philip's preaching and acts of power left even Simon openmouthed. He also became a Christian.

Philip enjoyed a great deal of popularity and success in sharing about Christ. Then, at the peak of the crusade, an angel of the Lord ordered him to leave Samaria and go south along a desert road to Gaza. Philip obeyed immediately.

Preaching on the Run

On the desert road Philip met a court official of an African queen in Ethiopia. The official managed the queen's bank roll and traveled frequently on business. This time, though, he had made the 1,200-mile trip to Jerusalem to worship the God of Israel. The lifeless formality of Judaism had probably turned off this spiritually hungry African.

When Philip spotted the chariot in the distance, the official was reading the Old Testament. God told Philip to hurry and join the man in his chariot.

Though he didn't have a pair of specially cushioned running sandals, Philip sprinted and caught up with the chariot. He explained to the official how Jesus Christ fulfilled the Old Testament prophecy of the coming Messiah. The official received Jesus as Saviour. Philip then baptized him in a pool of water that God provided in the desert. The Holy Spirit whisked Philip away and set him in the coastal city of Azotus. He continued preaching along the Mediterranean and elsewhere, taking the first step to expand the Christian church to non-Jews.

But success didn't go to Philip's head. He didn't hang around long enough to receive applause and pats on the back. Before the new converts became unhealthily attached to him, Philip left Samaria.

What was behind Philip's achievements? He let God take the wheel of his life and do the driving. He never became a backseat driver who second-guessed any road God took. Philip never considered obedience a burden. Let's focus on some important insights his story offers about obedience.

"Yes, God" (Grumble, Grumble)

It's funny how the same words can be heard in such different ways. A college teacher lectured about obedience to God through witnessing.

The lecture made Dave uncomfortable. He kept hearing a condemning negative command: "You *ought* to be witnessing, but you aren't!" Dave felt guilty because he hadn't shared his faith with anyone in quite a while. It bugged him that guys back in the dorm didn't know he was a Christian, but he didn't really want them to know. After the session on witnessing, Dave promised himself he'd try harder. He considered it was his responsibility as a Christian.

The same Sunday morning talk excited Susan. What she heard was, "God invites you to experience the joy of sharing Christ with others." The week before, Susan had led her roommmate to Jesus.

Both Dave and Susan thought of helping others know of Jesus' love as an act of obedience. For Dave, obedience seemed a crushing burden. Witnessing was something he felt he "ought" to do. For Susan, it was an opportunity, something she genuinely wanted to do.

When we think of obeying God, most of us have one of these two reactions. For some, God's commands mean a burden and guilt. For others, they mean opportunity and joy. What makes the difference?

Probably the best answer is that people see God and His "tone of voice" differently. If we see God as some faraway authority who constantly speaks in a "do this or else!" tone of voice, fear becomes the reason for what we do. We can't enjoy responding to words that always seem like demands. We're more likely to respond if we hear God's words in a framework of "invitation"—in a gentle tone of voice. We know God never acts or speaks contrary to His love for us. Won't you agree that it's harder to obey parents, coaches, and employers whose motives and love we question?

The only way we can hear the loving tone of God's voice is by trusting God's reasons for dropping "do" and "don't" commands on us. It doesn't imply that we'll always *feel* like obeying. (In fact, we may rather do anything but obey.) It means we realize that God has our best interests at heart.

God is loving. John declared, "This is how God showed his love among us: He sent His one and only Son into the world that we might live through Him. This is love: not that we loved God, but that He loved us and sent His Son as an atoning sacrifice for our sins" (1 John 4:9-10, NIV). Paul emphasized, "God demonstrates His own love for us in this: While we were still sinners, Christ died for us" (Romans 5:8, NIV).

Now we know the secret of Philip's unflinching obedience. He heard God speak in a gentle, inviting tone of voice. Convinced that God truly loved and valued him, he knew God had a good reason for giving what seemed to be a crazy command.

In his book *Love Is Now,* Peter Gillquist tells how a student's awareness of God's unconditional love increased his desire to obey:

A small group of us were addressing the members of a prominent social fraternity at UCLA. After the meeting, among several men who expressed their interest in knowing Jesus Christ was one young man who insisted he meet with someone in our group who would be available just as soon as possible.

Over coffee the following morning, he said, "I would give my eye teeth to have what you men have. But there's one thing holding me back."

"What's that?" my friend replied.

"Witnessing," he said.

"What do you mean?" we asked.

"I know good and well that if I give my heart to Christ, I'll have to start telling everyone I know how to get saved," he muttered.

"Where did you get that idea?"

"It's no idea. Some people I know who are Christians told me so. They said if you trust Christ, that's part of your responsibility, along with praying, reading the Bible, going to . . ."

"Just a minute," my friend interrupted. "God says He takes us as we are. It's strictly a matter of trusting Him. There are no price tags attached."

"Aw, come on," he objected. "You guys are out witnessing. What do you mean, you don't have to?"

"We're doing it because we *want* to. It's a tremendous thing to share the life of Christ with people, but that doesn't have a thing to do with becoming a Christian."

We went on to explain to him the greatness of God's love, and how at the cross, Jesus Christ so totally removed the barriers from him to God, that even if there were something he wanted to do to help deserve it, he couldn't.

"Are you telling me that I could accept

Jesus Christ right now, and never do a thing in return, and He'd still accept me?" he inquired, almost puzzled.

We assured him that was so.

"Well, if you *promise* me that Christ will come into my life today, and that I'll never have to witness, I'll accept Him."

"We promise," came our reply.

We prayed together, and he invited Jesus Christ to become his Lord and Saviour. We went on to explain to him that God had forgiven all sin—past, present, and future—everything he ever had or ever would do was placed upon Jesus Christ. We told him about his new life that would never end.

"This is the most fantastic thing I have ever heard," he responded. "I can't believe that I didn't have to do anything to get it."

He walked back over to the fraternity house. It was about 10:00 in the morning. He approached the first friend he saw and said, "I've got to tell you the most amazing thing I have ever heard. Today I realized that I could invite Jesus Christ to come into my life, and that I wouldn't have to witness or do anything, and He'd still come in. This is the greatest thing I have ever heard. Isn't that fantastic!" And by evening, he had spread the word around the entire fraternity. Because he didn't *have* to.

When we understand God's love, we realize God doesn't demand a goody-goody routine for us to gain His acceptance. A fear of rejection no longer drives us. We find freedom to obey because we realize that He doesn't expect the impossible. Obedience becomes a way of loving Him in return, and we start *wanting* to please Him in our actions.

John writes, "This is love for God: to obey His commands. And His commands are not burdensome, for everyone born of God has overcome the world" (1 John 5:3-4a, NIV). When we have a positive concept of God, we view His commands as an invitation to experience His very best.

To Obey God Is Not a *Natural* Response

The Bible says we can't be as perfect as God would like. We're inclined to disobey, to follow our selfish instincts rather than God's ways, even after we enter into a relationship with Jesus. But when we become Christians, the Holy Spirit works to help us in the struggle against sin. What some people call the "old" and "new" natures battle constantly for complete control of our lives. In every situation, we can choose to obey either of two urgings.

To forgive your dad for hitting your mom isn't a natural reaction. Neither is inviting to your party the girl who spread lies about you, or praying for that boring, uncaring math teacher, or memorizing Scripture in order to win over the lust that rules your thoughts.

Leaving Samaria abruptly wasn't Philip's *natural* response either. Most of us would have reacted something like this to the angel's instructions:

PHILIP: Go where? But that's just desert between Jerusalem and Gaza. Nobody lives there.

ANGEL: The Lord knows what He's doing, Philip. Just—

PHILIP: You don't understand. Tell God the Samaritans need me. Who will follow up this bunch of new believers?

ANGEL: Leave that to the Lord, Philip.

PHILIP: But this transfer doesn't make sense. Why is God doing it? What does He have up His sleeve? What kind of ministry can I have out in the middle of nowhere?

ANGEL: You'll see soon enough. Are you going or not?

PHILIP: OK, OK. But this looks like a demotion to me. Does God know how many converts we've had here in Samaria? You'd think I deserve better.

But Philip reacted *supernaturally* instead of naturally. He obeyed instantly, without complaint. Philip reminds us that obeying is a supernatural response to the Word of God, and to God's will as we discover it in our life.

The Power to Obey

God, some of Your commands are unbelievable.

Oh? For example?

You mean You expect me to love that teacher who embarrassed me in front of the whole class?

Yes.

To honor my parents, when their careers are

more important to them than me and my sisters?

Yes.

And You really expect me to keep my thought life pure in an X-rated environment?

Of course I do. Anything else?

Well, what about loving You? You really expect me to do that with all my heart, mind, and strength like the Bible says?

Yes.

But that caliber of life is awfully hard to achieve!

No, it isn't.

Hmmm! That's easy for You to say. You're God! You aren't saddled with what they call a "sinful nature." Look at this thing from *my* perspective.

I am. Obeying those commands isn't difficult. It's impossible!

Impossible? But why did You give us commands in the first place if You knew all along we couldn't obey them? What kind of game are You playing?

No game. Just My way of helping you realize your limitations. Admitting the impossibility of consistent obedience is the first step toward a more obedient life-style.

OK, so I admit I can't. But where does that leave me? Do we have to be less than Christians?

I'm glad you asked. My Son, Jesus, is the only Person who can live a successful Christian life. What's impossible for you is possible for Him. This isn't a pat answer—it's the only answer. Your ability to obey increases, depending on how close you are to Him. Power for living comes by trusting Him to help you do what you can't, and be what you aren't, on a one-day-at-a-time basis.

From Philip's example we understand the truth of that dialogue. He got his strength from being closer to Jesus and depending on Him. His conversation and preaching continually focused on Christ, not on vague doctrines or petty issues (Acts 8:5, 35). His ability to interpret the Old Testament prophecy for the Ethiopian showed that Philip regularly studied God's Word.

To put Philip on a pedestal because of his success at obeying would be a mistake. The source of power was God's, and Philip merely plugged into it.

Do You Have Spiritual Malnutrition?

A few years ago in Boston, the bodies of two elderly women were discovered in their small apartment. They had died a few days earlier. An autopsy revealed malnutrition was the cause of death. But hidden in the mattresses and sewn up in pillows and draperies was nearly $200,000 in cash! The ladies died because they didn't use what they had to meet their daily need for food.

We Christians have been given the abundance of the Holy Spirit, "who is able to do immeasurably more than all we ask or imagine" (Ephesians 3:20a, NIV).

Why some Christians live defeated lives and others live on top of things isn't because some have God's Spirit and some don't. The difference is that some are always aware of His presence and power, and others of us aren't. Some of us dare not relate to people, launch projects, or make decisions without seeking His help. Others of us clunk along on only one spiritual cylinder because we think we're capable of handling things on our own.

Paul sums up the problem of obedience. "We aren't saved from sin's grasp by knowing the commandments of God, because we can't and don't keep them, but God put into effect a different plan to save us. He sent His own Son in a human body like ours—except that ours are sinful—and destroyed sin's control over us by giving Himself as a sacrifice for our sins. So now we can obey God's laws if we follow after the Holy Spirit and no longer obey the old evil nature within us" (Romans 8:3-4, LB).

Having a relationship with God doesn't depend on whether or not we obey Him. Instead, our ability and desire to obey Him depends on the quality of our relationship with Him. If obedience feels like a burden, perhaps we should start letting Jesus carry some of the weight.

4
What's In a Name?

Your name is a tag that won't peel off or get lost. You've written it countless times on letters, on term papers, on Valentines, on job applications. In a crowded, buzzing hallway before the bell rings to start classes, your brain tunes out everything till someone calls your name. That single word perks up your senses and makes you feel important.

Why did your parents select your particular name?

Are you "Marie" because that's your mom's middle name? "Susan" because your mom has a close friend by that name? Is it "David Richards, Jr." because your dad likes the sound of his name? "Sonya" because it's unique? "Mike" because it's easy to pronounce?

Or did the literal meaning of the name sway your parents? For instance, "Dolly" means "gift from God." "John" comes from Hebrew and means "God is gracious." When parents select a name they don't usually know the literal meaning. But almost every name has a history and stands for something specific.

Even an uncommon or funny-sounding name can carry an important meaning. A good example is "Barnabas." Not many people you know have that name. Who wants to be called "Barney"? The name means "Son of Encouragement." A Barnabas is someone who often helps someone who's feeling down or confused.

Members of the first-century church in Jerusalem honored a man named Joseph by changing his name to Barnabas. What did Joseph do to earn the title of Encourager? How can we take part in the neglected but potential-packed ministry of encouragement?

Large Farm For Sale

Before Jesus returned to heaven, He told His disciples to travel and tell people about Him. Coming back after a preaching tour of Jerusalem's suburbs, this scene may have taken place as the disciples slumped into the chairs at a friend's house. Gloomy, tired expressions covered their faces.

"Whew, I'm exhausted!" Peter exclaimed. "Hiking across the desert makes me tired."

"Things wouldn't have been so bad if we hadn't run out of bread," Matthew said, catching his breath. "None of us has had a decent meal since we launched that last series of evangelistic services."

"And look at my sandals!" John complained. "The sand wore holes in 'em. I can't afford any new ones."

"One thing's for sure," Nathanael added. "We don't have the money it takes to keep preaching full-time. But Jesus told us to leave our jobs and spread the Gospel. What're we gonna do?"

Moments later Barnabas dropped in the room and greeted the disciples. "What're *you* doing here?" Andrew asked.

"Heard you fellows were here," Barnabas answered. "Look, I've got something for you." Barnabas dropped a huge roll of money on the coffee table. The disciples' eyes bulged out. They had never seen so much money at one time.

"What—what are you doing?" stammered Peter.

"God told me to sell my farm and give you the money," Barnabas said. "I figured church funds would be running low after that last campaign of yours. Now you can preach without worrying about your supplies."

Barnabas' unselfish deed (told in Acts 4:32-37) showed God's concern for others. Through Barnabas' gift, God was saying, "I haven't forgotten you. You can trust Me to meet your needs."

Barnabas viewed his possessions as God's property. He encouraged others by sacrificing and sharing.

A Good Word for Paul

As a leading Jewish official in Jerusalem, Paul came down hard on Christianity. He thought it ridiculous to say that Jesus was God's Son. He felt he should put believers behind bars, and he gave his hearty OK to at least one execution. Paul headed a group that left for Damascus with the aim of rounding up Christians and persecuting them. But on the way, Jesus Himself came up to Paul and scolded him for persecuting His followers. Paul's views about Jesus changed right then.

So radical was Paul's change of mind that he began preaching about Jesus in Damascus. Then, back in Jerusalem, he tried to join a band of Jesus' followers. But tempers flared.

"No way can Paul join our group!" insisted one follower. "I don't think he's really a Christian. Not long ago he was our No. 1 enemy."

"Yeah. Maybe he's claiming to be Christian so he can destroy the church from inside," suggested another follower. "I'm not falling for his sneaky scheme."

"I'm afraid of him," a third said. "He's the same man who agreed with the stoning of our friend Stephen."

Paul's conversion to Christianity was for real, but few Christians believed his 180-degree turn. Their aloof attitude, and an attempt by bitter Jews to kill him, may have discouraged Paul. No longer accepted by either group, he probably had that "what's-the-use" feeling. Many new Christians have shucked their faith in similar circumstances.

That's when Barnabas stood up for him. He personally introduced Paul to the disciples in Jerusalem and told them about Paul's talk with

Jesus. Barnabas backed up Paul's testimony. "Give him a break," Barnabas pleaded. "Don't judge the man on the basis of his past."

Thanks to Barnabas' influence, Paul worked with the disciples in Jerusalem and led many people to believe in Jesus. Three years later, Barnabas recruited Paul to teach a group of new converts in Antioch. Later still, Paul engaged in missionary work and helped bring thousands to Christianity. Of course, God also inspired him and looked over his shoulder as he wrote the letters that became part of the Bible.

Barnabas never kept pace with Paul's education, abilities, or number of people he converted. By the time the first century approached its midpoint, Paul's fame had mushroomed. Barnabas remained in obscurity. Still, Barnabas was instrumental in all that God accomplished through Paul. His words and deeds of encouragement never made him a household name, but they were behind Paul's best efforts for Christ. Barnabas' hand in Paul's achievements shows the powerful potential of encouragement. Paul received the publicity. Paul expanded the geographical borders of Christianity. Paul is the name we remember. But without Barnabas, there might never have been a Paul!

Blue-sky Barnabas

Jerusalem had the only Christian church till persecution of believers began. Then Christians began traveling in all directions, sharing their faith as they went. In places such as Phoenicia,

Cyprus, and Antioch, new churches sprang up. The church in Antioch welcomed Greeks as well as converted Jews. These Greeks had no training in the Old Testament nor did they keep to a strict moral code. Their participation in church activities raised eyebrows back in Jerusalem. Because of this, Barnabas went to Antioch to check things out.

Christians in Antioch weren't carbon copies of Jerusalem believers. They probably worshiped in a slightly different way. But these differences didn't disturb Barnabas. He didn't force the new church to be just like the Jerusalem fellowship. He didn't go nit-picking about weaknesses that he undoubtedly saw. He didn't sling mud at their methods.

Instead, "When he arrived and saw the wonderful things God was doing, he was filled with excitement and joy, and encouraged the believers to stay close to the Lord, whatever the cost. Barnabas was a kindly person, full of the Holy Spirit and strong in faith. As a result large numbers of people were added to the Lord" (Acts 11:23-24, LB).

A pessimist would have turned a suspicious eye toward the church in Antioch and expected a breakup between Jewish and Greek members. Not Barnabas. He talked up the good in the Greek church and spread enthusiasm for what God was doing in the people's lives. The Antioch Christians sent Barnabas and Paul for a year to the mission field, to areas previously untouched by Christianity.

Blue-sky Bill

Barnabas reminds me of a fellow nicknamed "Blue-sky Bill." He works for a youth ministry organization. Trying to solve people's problems seven days a week gives Bill more than his share of frustration and pressure. Every year he runs into scores of emotionally scarred teens and messed-up families. That kind of experience would make many people cynical and discouraged.

Not Bill. He keeps praising God for the small percentage of changed lives and mended homes out of all those he meets. He focuses on the good that happens, rather than on the bad that sometimes wins out. Bill constantly expects God to do something bigger and better in his life and work. He encourages people around him with back-slapping greetings and timely compliments. He draws out the best in his friends by praising the best in their character and work.

Impersonalism, deceit, and despair flood our world. We need more "Blue-sky Barnabases" who can see the positive in people and in circumstances.

A Second Chance
for John Mark

If Barnabas hadn't seen the good that John Mark could do for the Church, Mark wouldn't have had a chance to do anything. Paul didn't want to take Mark along on his trip. But Barnabas risked his reputation and gave Mark a second try. He encouraged Mark by forgiving past failures and by

Missionary Team Breaks Up

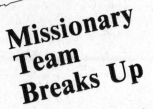

ANTIOCH (AP)—Missionaries Paul and Barnabas have split over a personnel dispute, reliable Antioch church sources report.

The break came after Barnabas suggested bringing John Mark, former deserter from a missionary expedition, along on their upcoming trip. Paul refused and departed with an aide.

"He kept talking about how young and immature Mark was," said Barnabas in Cyprus. Barnabas pointed to Mark's potential as a leader as a factor in his decision to defend the young Mark.

However, Paul cited the extreme danger of harassment and stonings which have plagued Christian evangelists in his stand to bar Mark from further missionary work.

Some church leaders expressed guarded satisfaction over the breakup. As one said, "Now we have two teams of workers instead of one."

drawing out his potential. Barnabas' risk paid off! Years later, Mark assisted Peter in Rome. Paul's view of Mark also changed. Writing from prison shortly before his death, Paul told Timothy, "Pick up Mark and bring him with you, for he is useful to me for service" (1 Timothy 4:11b, NASB). Mark wrote the Gospel that bears his name, an account of Jesus' life that God is still using to convert people to Christianity.

All because Barnabas didn't give up on him!

How to Multiply Yourself

Barnabas' encouragement multiplied the efforts of the Jerusalem and Antioch churches and made the most of Paul's and John Mark's abilities. No sermon ever preached, no religious book ever written besides the Bible, no hymn ever composed has had as enduring an impact on history as the behind-the-scenes things Barnabas did to encourage people. When Christ measures our potential, He looks not just at our own abilities, but at the acts of people we can help. Few people can duplicate Paul and Mark's contributions. But everyone can be a Barnabas. Here's how:

By sharing material resources. This involves sacrificing and giving to promote the work of Christ in the world, and sharing with individuals who have less. God wants to use our money to tell others about His concern.

By forgiving others' mistakes, and not judging them on the basis of past failures. Thinking of how often we've blown it in the past makes it easier to forgive others. By giving people fresh chances, we make it easier for them to forgive themselves.

By giving timely words of support or praise. Flattery is an insincere compliment coming from a selfish motive. Praise is an *earned* compliment. After all, no one enjoys feeling taken for granted.

By reminding a defeated, discouraged person of his potential. Failure can cripple our emotions. Helping a person focus on his strengths can restore his self-confidence. Do we have faith in God's ability to change the most unlikely of people?

By spending time with individuals who feel alone, or need a listening ear. Nothing builds a person's self-esteem like another's seeing him in person. In order to do this well, we need to be sensitive to people we meet—even if they aren't popular or attractive. It means being willing to give of ourselves to help them feel wanted.

By growing in our faith and developing our character. Nobody's perfect. But others will notice sincere efforts to weave together our faith and our life. Our applied love for Jesus may nudge onlookers into considering Jesus Christ as a way of life.

By developing a happy, optimistic disposition. God maintains ultimate control over history. Evil and suffering are temporary and followers of Jesus have the only legitimate reason for optimism. "For whatever is born of God overcomes the world; and this is the victory that has overcome the world—our faith. And who is the one who overcomes the world, but he who believes that Jesus is the Son of God?" (1 John 5:4-5, NASB).

"Barnabas" is no longer a popular name. But your name doesn't have to mean "encourager" in order for you to be one!

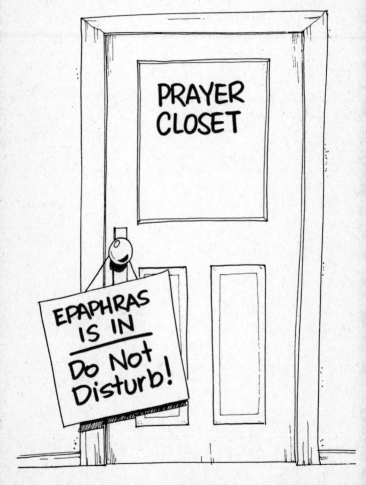

5
Positive Gossip

I'll never forget Floyd's phone call. It came the week I was wrestling with a tough decision about a new job. Through a mutual friend, Floyd had learned of the problem facing me. From 2,000 miles away he assured me, "Terry, I love you as a brother, and I'll be praying for you every day till you reach a decision."

Stan will never forget one evening during his junior year of college. His studying was interrupted by the news of his dad's serious heart attack. Stan started immediately for the hospital. The doctors didn't expect his dad to live through the night. Stan found out later—as his dad was recovering—that his roommate had stayed awake all that night praying for his dad.

Greg dreaded the final exam in chemistry. He needed a good grade to pass the course. As he studied on the night of the exam, anxiety kept sapping his energy and wrecking his concentration. Then Charlie called. Knowing Greg felt uptight about the exam, Charlie prayed with him over the phone. Charlie's prayer didn't guarantee Greg a good grade, but Greg felt more relaxed just knowing someone cared.

Floyd, Stan's roommate, and Charlie are Christians who spend time talking to God about the needs of their friends. To them, the declaration "I'll pray for you!" is no meaningless cliché. A cliché is a phrase or expression used so frequently and carelessly that it loses its meaning. In a recent discussion group, I asked 20 college students to brainstorm for a list of the most often-used Christian clichés. "I'll pray for you" easily got the most votes. When we hear someone say those words, we wonder if he'll follow through. The prayers—not those easy words—are what can help us.

Example of Positive Gossip

A little-known first-century Christian named Epaphras didn't say, "I'll pray for you" without meaning it. By looking at his life, we can learn about the ministry of "positive gossip." (*Positive* gossip is talking about friends behind their backs—to God!)

The life of Epaphras doesn't fill much space in the New Testament, but Paul mentioned him in the first and fourth chapters of Colossians, as well as in Philemon.

Epaphras had been converted under Paul's ministry in Ephesus a few years before; then he returned to his hometown of Colossae. There he began sharing his faith and started a church. While Paul was in a Rome prison, Epaphras gave him a progress report on the church. Paul responded to the report with the Book of Colossians.

Epaphras and Paul were close friends, since Paul called him "beloved" and a "fellow bond-servant" (Colossians 1:7). Paul also called him "my fellow prisoner in Christ Jesus" (Philemon 23), indicating that Epaphras was in prison with Paul. He was either in prison with Paul voluntarily, or like Paul, he had been taken captive for spreading the Gospel. Consistency and self-sacrifice marked his life-style, for Paul also called him "a faithful servant of Christ on our behalf" (Colossians 1:7, NASB).

It is interesting that Epaphras' influence on the believers in Colossae didn't lessen when he left for Rome to visit Paul. In his letter, Paul said, "Epaphras ... sends you his greetings, always laboring earnestly for you in his prayers, that you may stand perfect and fully assured in all the will of God. For I bear him witness that he had a deep concern for you" (Colossians 4:12-13, NASB).

From a closer look at this comment of Paul's, we learn that praying for others is as important as preaching, teaching, singing, or witnessing. Let's take a look at our prayer life in light of the following principles from Colossians 4:12-13.

Prayer is hard work. Epaphras was "always

laboring earnestly" for the Colossians. In other words, whether or not he prayed didn't hinge on his up and down feelings. Epaphras didn't approach God just when he felt spiritual or was on an emotional high. He disciplined himself to pray!

For years I've been jogging. No matter how tired I am at the end of the day, I jog a couple miles. Often jogging is the last thing I feel like doing, but because I know it helps me, I do it. Recently God reminded me that if I can jog when I don't feel like it, I can pray for others even when I'm not in the mood. I became sensitive to Paul's words to Timothy: "Take time and trouble to keep yourself spiritually fit. Bodily fitness has a limited value, but spiritual fitness is of unlimited value, for it holds promise both for this present life and for the life to come!" (1 Timothy 4:8, PH).

The maturity of your Christian friends depends in part on you. Though you come to Christ individually, you grow as part of a group through your relationships with other Christians. Comparing the church to a human body, Paul wrote, "Under [Christ's] direction the whole body is fitted together perfectly, and each part in its own special way helps the other parts, so that the whole body is healthy and growing and full of love" (Ephesians 4:16, LB).

A 17-year-old from Newport News, Va. told me, "The people in my church were only interested in getting me saved. The day I signed a card and joined the church they forgot about me. Whether or not I grow as a Christian doesn't seem to matter."

In his book *How Do I Fit In?*, Larry Richards says, "God knows that living the Christian life, sharing our faith with non-Christians, and working out our problems is far beyond our own ability. So He's provided help. He's planned for a truly interdependent relationship between believers."

Jesus didn't take His disciples' spiritual development for granted. He knew that praying for them was just as important as teaching them. Jesus asked God the Father to give the Holy Spirit to His disciples (John 14:16). He prayed specifically for Peter, so that his faith would not fail (Luke 22:32). Jesus also prayed for the disciples' unity, joy, and fruitful service (John 17:6-19, 21-26). If it was necessary to keep men like Peter, James, John and Matthew going through prayer, it's even more necessary to follow Jesus' example and talk to God about our Christian friends.

Prayer is one of the many ways we can help our friends mature. Let's not take their spiritual development for granted. They need us.

Prayer should be rooted in genuine concern for the other person. Paul assured the Colossians that Epaphras had a deep concern for them (Colossians 4:13). His concern suggests that Epaphras had friendships with the Colossians, which made him sensitive to their personal needs. It implies too that the promise "I'll pray for you" never became just a meaningless cliché to Epaphras.

Positive Gossip in Action

A few years ago a song titled "Easier Said than Done" became a hit. It's as true about prayer as about anything else. We find it easier to talk about it and study it than to do it! But knowing the importance of helping others through prayer is no guarantee we'll follow through. To help you make prayer a habit, here are some ideas.

Don't put off your prayers. We may mean it when we promise to pray for someone, but often we forget an hour or a day later. If you recognize a friend's need while chatting on the phone, stop and pray together, or say a short prayer the instant you hang up. When you yell to someone in the hallway at school, "I'll pray for you," you may decide to wait till you have a block of time to pray. But seldom do we have the time. We have to *make* time. So say a prayer for that person as you walk to your next class. God hears a 30-second prayer just as clearly as a five-minute one.

Writer Charlie Shedd explained how he prays the second he becomes aware of the need. "I have little cues. When the phone rings, I pray that I'll be able to serve whoever is on the line ... if the doorbell rings, that's a cue to pray for the person I'm going to meet in a second. Whenever I hear a siren, I try to think of the people who need help right that second and pray for them."

Learn to use chunks of time in which you're physically active, but mentally free. Praying for friends while we're busy at something doesn't mean we're slighting them. It's good use of time.

If Epaphras were around today, he'd probably pray for friends while driving to school, jogging, bagging groceries, and washing the car.

Keep a prayer journal. In a loose leaf notebook or composition book, make these vertical column headings:

Date	Request	How God Answered	Date of Answer

Jot down both the need you share with God, and how He responds to it later—even if you don't get the answer you expected. After a couple weeks, look over your entries. You'll be surprised how consistently God steps in for you. Of course, you can put personal requests in this journal as well as requests for others.

A girl in Phoenix explained what keeping a journal means to her: "I was having trouble praying, so to improve my concentration I began recording the date of each request, the date God answered, and how He answered. When I'm discouraged, it's a faith-builder to flip through the journal and remember God's faithfulness in the past. It's like a time capsule. You forget what you write in it, but when you flip through it you remember how good God is."

Start a prayer request bulletin board. One guy I know has seven letter-sized envelopes pinned to his bulletin board. On each envelope he has printed a day of the week. As he becomes aware of a friend's need, he writes a prayer request on a 3″ x 5″ card with the person's name at the top and puts it in one of the envelopes. Each evening, he looks over the cards in that day's envelope and prays specifically for those requests. This lets him pray at least once a week for each person. He throws the note cards away when the need no longer exists, and writes more requests on a card when a person's need changes.

Try to set aside a time and place to pray just for others. Sue sets her alarm 10 minutes early and "gossips positively" to begin the day. Brad reserves 5 or 10 minutes in the school library for silent prayer. Rick prays for friends while training for cross-country meets. What time and place is best for prayer? Nobody can answer that for you, but there are advantages in reserving the same time and place every day.

But when you do fail to keep your prayer time, don't feel all shot down. Modern pressures make it tough to keep schedules. God loves us even when we neglect praying for others. We have to accept our weaknesses and admit them to God.

From Epaphras, we learn that prayer doesn't just prepare us to serve Christ. Prayer for others *is* Christian service! Because Epaphras is directly referred to in only five Bible verses, we discover that *what* is said about us matters more than *how much* is said about us. We can't all be great teachers or singers or writers, but we can be behind-the-scenes servants who quietly help change the world through prayer.

"Ten Ways to Witness Painlessly"

The ten ways are:

- ☐ 1. Wear your perfect attendance Sunday School award pin to school.
- ☐ 2. Carry your family's 2' x 3' family Bible to school with you.
- ☐ 3. Slip tracts in lockers, bathrooms, teachers' lounge, principal's office, lunchroom...
- ☐ 4. Put religious bumper stickers all over your car (or bicycle or motorcycle or skateboard).
- ☐ 5. Ask a stranger for directions, then give him "directions" to heaven.
- ☐ 6. Wear witnessing jewelry: cross necklace, resurrection belt buckle, baptism shoelaces, Jesus patches, John 3:16 comb...
- ☐ 7. Leave your Romans 3:23 inscribed pencil lying on your desk and hope it gets ripped off.
- ☐ 8. Hand a tract that explains the plan of salvation to an unsaved friend, then stand back and look religious while she reads it.
- ☐ 9. Let Christ's living through your life show your friends that being a Christian really does make a difference.
- ☐ 10. Learn to really care about people as Christ did with his friends and enemies.

From Witnessing, Inc.

6
Why Didn't You Tell Me Before?

SUSAN: Everybody in church says you ought to witness, but nobody does it very much!

MARCIA: I can't get up the courage to do it, but I know I should. I'm afraid I won't know what to say.

FRANK: I've really tried to tell others about Jesus, but I seem to turn people off. It makes me want to quit trying.

MARK: I don't think a person has to talk about Jesus. Isn't it enough just to lead a good life?

NANCY: I once thought witnessing was easy. But that was when I only thought about witnessing and never did it!

KATHY: There are so many groups peddling their own brand of evangelism that I get confused. I wonder which one works best.

Sharing what Jesus means to us isn't automatic or easy. It's more than carrying a Bible to school, or leaving a tract along with our tip. It's not only knocking on strangers' doors in the middle of their favorite cops-and-robbers program, or pasting a "Honk if you love Jesus" bumper sticker on a car.

A witness is more than a slicked-up dude with the fastest Bible in town, who can shoot you down with Scripture from Genesis to Revelation.

Scripture exposes how shallow these ideas of a sharing life-style are, and describes the person who makes the grade as a witness. In this chapter, we can't tell all of what Scripture says about personal evangelism. But we can look at the life of a man who practiced it and find practical guidelines for ourselves in how to share.

Andrew *Who?*

That's a common reaction when someone mentions his name. Andrew isn't as familiar as many other Bible characters. A Jew from Galilee, his name meant "manliness." He and his brother, Peter, owned part of a fishing business in Capernaum and lived together.

Though he was one of Jesus' Twelve Disciples, Andrew never stood out. Unlike Matthew and John, Andrew never wrote a book of the Bible. He doesn't have sermons or miracles recorded in the book of Acts as other followers do. What he said or did didn't rate much attention in his time.

Andrew lived in the shadow of his gifted older brother. Peter's words and actions dot the four Gospels and Acts. Not Andrew's. Only three times in the New Testament does he appear in action. Peter delivered one sermon that God used to convert 3,000 persons. Andrew didn't. Peter wrote two letters that became a part of Scripture. Andrew didn't. The church at Jerusalem accepted Peter as a leader of the apostles. Andrew didn't share that spotlight.

During after-church socials, Andrew probably heard remarks like, "What's your name again? Oh yes, you're Peter's brother!" Twice, New Testament authors described him as "Peter's brother" (Matthew 10:2 and John 6:8)—as if it weren't enough just to be Andrew!

It's easy to remember Peter, and easy to forget Andrew. If we had walked in Andrew's sandals, how would we have felt? Inferior? Would we have compared ourselves with Peter and the other disciples and felt useless to God? Would we have gone around saying, "I can't" and "Let somebody else do it"?

Andrew's life is worth looking at because as far as we can tell from Scripture, he didn't complain, compare, or feel useless. He probably sized up his good and bad points, and used what he had for Jesus.

Though it's Peter we usually remember, it was Andrew who brought Peter to Christ. John the Baptist's preaching attracted Andrew (John 1:29-42). John publicly identified Jesus as the Son of God, the long-awaited Jewish Messiah. Their curiosity aroused, Andrew and a friend stayed with Jesus for a day. Andrew became convinced of Jesus' identity and rushed to tell Peter. Then he took his brother to meet Jesus.

Andrew was the first person who followed Jesus as the Son of God after John revealed who He was. He was also the first to win another to Jesus.

Days later, Jesus told the brothers to give up their fishing business and devote themselves full-time to His service. "Come, follow Me! And I will make you fishermen for the souls of men!" (Mark 1:17, LB).

Andrew acted again when he brought to Jesus a boy whose five barley loaves and two fish Jesus used to feed 5,000 men, plus women and children (John 6:1-14). Even Andrew doubted the usefulness of the boy's meal. But Jesus' miracle was like Andrew's own life in Jesus' hands. Jesus can turn a little into a lot. What counts is availability—not just ability.

Andrew appears for the third time during the last week of Jesus' public ministry in Jerusalem. As Jesus taught in the temple, several Greeks approached Philip asking to see Jesus. Philip talked to Andrew about bringing the Greeks to Jesus and they finally decided to tell Jesus about them. (A wall of prejudice kept Jews and Greeks apart. The disciples probably were uptight about how the public would react if Jesus welcomed Greeks near the Jewish temple during their Passover holiday.)

Andrew's career isn't well-known, but that doesn't lessen the value of his life. According to legend, Andrew spent his final years in Greece. An official whose wife had been influenced by Andrew's preaching had him crucified.

Applying Andrew

What does Andrew's story tell us?

Only knowing Jesus personally qualifies us to introduce others to Him. We never stop a stranger in a shopping center and begin introducing him to a friend we have along. It's equally absurd to try to introduce friends to Jesus if we haven't ourselves entered into a relationship with Him.

Talk show hosts often read press clippings about people who will be on their shows. But they still meet these guests backstage before introducing them to the audience. They know there's a crucial difference between knowing *about* a person and knowing him.

Andrew's conversion shows the process we have to go through to become an effective witness. First, Andrew's loyalty to John the Baptist reveals his spiritual hunger. He spent a day with Jesus to learn more. What Andrew learned planted in him a deep belief in Jesus as the Son of God. Sharing his experience of Christ with Peter was the natural outcome of hunger, learning, and belief.

A 16-year-old girl who prayed to receive Christ on the final day of a crusade remarked, "I had tried to share my faith all week with a visitation team from our youth group. I wondered why it was so difficult and uncomfortable for me to share the Gospel. Now I know why. It's pretty hard to talk about something you've never experienced."

An attitude of willingness is more useful to God than your being super-talented. Andrew understood that his usefulness to Christ didn't depend on how his gifts and skills compared with those of other disciples. Thinking that God only uses attractive, popular, multitalented individuals is wrong. Often we serve Christ best in a position of weakness rather than strength.

Mary cheated on Mr. Cook's chemistry exam. That evening, haunted by guilt, she confessed to her father. "You need to tell Mr. Cook," her dad insisted.

"But I can't do that!" Mary said. "He isn't a Christian, but he knows I am. What will he think if I tell him I cheated?"

The next day, following her dad's orders, she confessed to Mr. Cook. "I want you to lower my grade or—or—something," Mary stammered. "And forgive me for what I did."

She nervously waited for a response. He said, "Mary, I've taught for three years, and you're the first student who has asked forgiveness for cheating. You're the first example of a real Christian I've seen on this campus!"

Never underestimate the long-range effect of leading a person to Jesus. When Andrew led Peter to Jesus, he didn't know that his brother would become a great church leader. What we can do for Christ isn't limited to just what we ourselves can do, but also what those we bring to Christ accomplish.

In 1858, a Sunday School teacher named Mr. Kimball led a Boston clerk to Christ. That clerk, Dwight L. Moody, became an evangelist. In 1879, in a crusade in England, Moody challenged

a complacent pastor named Frederick B. Meyer.
Later, Meyer's speech at an American college
brought to Christ a student, J. Wilbur Chapman.
Chapman, engaged in YMCA work, employed a
former baseball player, Billy Sunday, to do
evangelistic work. Sunday held a crusade in
Charlotte, N. C. Its success inspired a second
crusade, led by Mordecai Ham. In Ham's
crusade, Billy Graham became a Christian.

Could Mr. Kimball possibly know what he
started?

*A personal relationship is the most effective
way to share Christ.* When we get to know a
non-Christian and demonstrate unconditional
concern over a period of time, we earn the right
to be heard. Andrew's witness to Peter had credibility because Peter knew and respected him.

Some Christians purposefully keep a distance
between themselves and non-Christian
classmates and co-workers. They insist it's biblical to remain separated from an unbelieving
world. But separation from the world doesn't
mean isolation from the people of the world.
Being with non-Christians should never be an
excuse for us to lower our standards. But we can't
reach the world for Christ without building relationships with unbelievers. Jesus sent His disciples into the world, and prayed to God the
Father, "I'm not asking You to take them out of
the world, but to keep them safe from Satan's
power" (John 17:15, LB). The insulation of God's
Spirit can protect us from potentially evil
influences.

A beautiful flower, the lily, grows best in mud. A chemical substance within the flower keeps mud from clinging to its petals. The flower keeps its natural beauty in spite of its muddy environment. We should not be separated from our environment, but from the unchristian nature of that environment.

Word-of-mouth sharing should complement your actions as a Christian. Andrew aroused Peter's interest with words, not just with a difference in life-style.

Jean says, "I concentrated on living a good, silent life, hoping that through my actions alone friends would want to trust Christ. But they never brought up the subject of Jesus. They merely thought I was a 'do-gooder' since I refused to go along with some of their activities. Over a period of time our friendship weakened and they never knew I was trying to witness for Jesus through my actions. I learned that unless I verbalize the Gospel, my 'do-good' life only draws attention to myself."

José Pagan played shortstop for the San Francisco Giants in the 1962 World Series. In one game, Bobby Richardson, New York Yankee second baseman, doubled. José recalls: "I was playing back, close to second, when I heard Bobby call 'José!' What could a Yankee player want with me in the middle of a heated World Series game? I knew that Bobby was a Christian, but I couldn't think of a reason why he would call my name except to confuse me.

"'Hey, José!' Bobby called again, 'I want to

know—do you really know the Lord?'

" 'Yes,' I said, nodding to my Christian brother. I had received Christ only a short time before the Series. Though I tried to concentrate on the rest of the ballgame, I kept seeing Bobby's face and hearing his voice. There he was, a great player, in the middle of baseball's most exciting contest, asking me if I knew the Lord! Our team lost the Series, but I gained something of lasting value. I learned that I'm never too busy to talk about Jesus."

Andrew's recruitment of Peter shows what witnessing is: the spontaneous overflow of a life excited about Jesus. Andrew wanted his brother to share his discovery. Witnessing isn't a way of earning God's love or proving we're Christians. It's a response of love to what God has done. Sharing is a natural response to someone who enjoys growing close to Christ. Let's share because we *want* to, not because we feel we *ought* to.

This definition of witnessing also teaches us what to say to non-Christians. We begin by sharing things God has done for us, prayers He has answered, goals He has re-directed, how we felt before we received Christ.

Jesus healed a blind man. The Pharisees—enemies of Jesus—interrogated the man. "Give the glory to God, but not to Jesus," they said. "Jesus is an evil person." The once-blind man didn't have a lot of smart answers. He simply said, "I don't know whether He is good or bad, ... but I know this: *I was blind, and now I see!*" (John 9:25, LB). Becoming a theologian isn't necessary for witnessing. Bible knowledge increases effectiveness, but anyone whom Christ has blessed can qualify.

Whether or not we introduce Christ to our friends is a test of our love for Him. Andrew's contacts with Peter, the small boy, and the Greeks demonstrated his love for Jesus as well as his concern for them.

Francine was the first girl I dated regularly. We attended colleges 30 miles apart. Most Saturday nights we had fun going to dinner or to a miniature golf course. At least I was enjoying seeing her. One evening I found out that I wasn't as important to her as I thought.

During the graduation ceremonies at her college, I sat with Barbara, Francine's hometown friend. At the reception, Barbara and I followed Francine around as she said good-bye to a circle of teachers. Francine excitedly introduced Barbara to every instructor. She introduced me only once, saying, "Oh, yes. This is so and so from Wingate College." If we really love Christ, introducing Him to others won't just come as an afterthought.

Stuart Briscoe explained why sitting back and playing with our halos isn't enough in a world of spiritual hunger. "We have conditioned ourselves into thinking that all that really matters is that we should be good, honest, clean-living, churchgoing Christians. Now with all due respect, that's a cop-out. There are going to be souls in hell who are convinced you were a good, clean-living, churchgoing Christian, and they'll be in hell because they never heard that the Gospel is relevant to them.

"Evangelism is not the added extra for those who are that-way inclined. The church is in the world's debt. I'm alarmed by the philosophy that the sole task of the church is to turn out nice Christian people. I believe the sole task of the church is to turn out people who honestly believe they have the only message of hope and that they are the only people who have it."

Fear of failure or rejection often keeps us from sharing our faith. But people are more receptive than we think.

For two years, I had a crush on a high school cheerleader. Between classes, I tagged behind her up and down the halls. I told friends how I felt about her, and stuffed mushy poems in her locker. Yet I didn't have the nerve to speak to her face to face. I was afraid she'd give me the brush-off.

Then one afternoon I spotted her standing alone by her locker. I overcame wobbly knees and erratic heartbeats long enough to tell her how I felt. She stared at me for a moment, then asked wide-eyed, "Why didn't you tell me this before?"

That's what some unbelievers say when they finally hear the Good News of Christ. God uses "average" players like Andrew as well as superstars like Peter to do the work of Christ.

James

7

How to Be Your Own Boss

People have a terrible urge to control other people and things.

Wars are started because one nation wants to control another country's people and natural resources. Through hypnotism, people can control the minds of others. Birth control pills are used to limit the human population. Advertisers sway the buying habits of radio listeners and television viewers. We invent complex machinery and appliances that respond to the turn of a knob or to the push of a button. We've gained mastery over the earth's raw materials, letting us produce fuel, develop fast transportation, and build skyscrapers.

In spite of all our abilities to control other people and technology, *self*-control is still one of our biggest problems. The kingdom hardest to rule is the kingdom of ourselves!

TOM: I don't care much for homework. It bugs

me the way some teachers load it on, especially over weekends. There are a whole bunch of other things I'd rather be doing than studying.

WARREN: I know it would help me, but I can't seem to make myself sit down and study the Bible!

CAROL: I often go to my first class bleary-eyed from watching the late show the night before. I tell myself I'll just watch the first part, but I wind up crawling into bed past midnight.

DAVE: I usually pray just when I feel like it, and my feelings aren't too consistent.

DIANE: I'm the type that can just look at food and gain weight! I start a new diet every month, but can't stay on any of them.

ED: Disciplining my emotions is hard for me. I'm quick-tempered with my folks, and when I'm out with my girlfriend, it's pretty hard to, you know, keep control.

ROGER: I'm always getting caught saying something I shouldn't, or just saying something period—something that I kind of suspect nobody really wants to hear. I must have been born with a big mouth!

Success in studies, sports, personal relationships, business—in any area of living—demands self-discipline. It helps us reach our potential in Christian living. Former Wheaton College president V. Raymond Edman said, "Discipleship means discipline. Without discipline we are not disciples, even though we profess His name and pass for followers of Jesus."

What does the Bible say about self-discipline?

What practical insights about developing this quality does it offer? Is our weakness and wishy-washiness there forever, or is change possible? One way the Bible answers these questions is through the life of James, Jesus' half-brother. Let's get to know James and see what his story tells us about improving our self-discipline.

Better Late than Never

Some authorities say Jesus had at least six younger brothers and sisters. Imagine living under the same roof with the only perfect brother who ever lived! How would that make you feel?

Carpentry work didn't put James' family in a high-income bracket. Home life in Nazareth was simple but deeply religious for members of this Jewish family.

At first, none of Jesus' four brothers believed He was the Messiah promised in the Old Testament. One time, they publicly sneered at Him. They visited Capernaum looking for Jesus, perhaps concerned that His radical teaching would give the family a bad name.

Things changed after the Resurrection, when Jesus appeared to James. James' views about his brother changed instantly! He didn't keep his fresh belief to himself either. Jesus' other three brothers—probably at James' urging—attended a prayer meeting in Jerusalem right after Jesus' ascension into heaven.

God selected James for a leadership position in the local church in Jerusalem. Paul, three years after his dramatic conversion, talked with James in Jerusalem. James helped Paul piece together details of Jesus' life and ministry.

After Paul's first missionary journey, James led a church meeting about Gentiles' coming into the Christian church. Many Christian Jews felt that in order to become a church member, people of other races and nationalities should start obeying the Jewish laws. But James insisted that the church spare non-Jews the religious laws that governed Jews. James strictly obeyed the laws and customs of Judaism. But as a Christian he understood that faith in Jesus' death and resurrection—not works—gave people a relationship with God.

According to one legend, in A.D. 62, bitter scribes and Pharisees, who considered James a traitor to Judaism, tossed him off a pinnacle of the temple of Jerusalem, a sheer drop of several hundred feet. Then they stoned him to death.

If you're wondering how self-discipline fits into James' saga, hold on.

James, the Man of Steel Will

James, according to tradition, took a Nazarite vow, a strict means of separating himself from the world for a period of time. While under the vow, James stopped doing a lot of things, such as drinking wine, shaving, and eating meat. The vow was a unique way in which God tested men whom He wanted to use as spiritual leaders. Keeping the vow required rigid self-control.

Another sign of James' self-discipline is his

nickname, meaning "camel's knees." He knelt in prayer so often and for so long that the skin over his knees became hardened like a camel's.

Probably the earliest New Testament book to be written was his five-chapter letter, James. In the letter, James encouraged a practical Christian life-style that, apart from self-discipline, is impossible to maintain. He wrote about nitty-gritty aspects of living, about works that genuine faith in Jesus should produce. The following topics in his letter show the need for self-discipline:

—responding joyfully to trials (1:2-5; 5:7-13)

—maintaining an active prayer life (1:5; 4:2-3; 5:13-18)

—saying "no" to temptation to sin (1:13-15, 27; 4:7)

—controlling the tongue (1:19-20; 3:2-12; 4:11; 5:9, 12)

—studying and applying Scripture (1:21-25)

—compassionate use of money (5:1-6)

James implies that an undisciplined Christian isn't as happy or useful as he should be. However, just seeing James' positive example doesn't help us much. In fact, as we look at our weak selves in comparison, we often feel frustrated and discouraged. What ideas can we glean from his life and writing that can give us a handle on the problem?

An Inside Job

No area of life can flourish without self-discipline. James' Nazarite vow involved rigid limits on his social and physical life. God doesn't intend that we should all impose the same re-strictions on ourselves, but what we do in these areas is due to self-control. James' long hours in prayer and Old Testament study required com-mand of his faculties and an uncanny ability to concentrate. James' letter to Jewish Christians demonstrates the benefit of self-discipline in communication among people. (Few people enjoy writing. Most of us only enjoy having done it! That's why our unanswered letters pile up and we start our term papers the evening before they're due.)

James' written instructions concerning the tongue and temper show the necessity of putting a leash on our emotions. The life-style God calls for through James' pen involves discipline of our actions (things we initiate), our reactions to people and circumstances, our thoughts and at-titudes, our time, our values (things we deem important), as well as our feelings.

Whether it's music lessons or cheerleading practice, forgiving someone or having devotions, or refusing that extra slice of pizza, we need discipline!

Leading an emotionally oriented, impulsive life-style is useless. Emotions are temporary and inconsistent. God gives us a kaleidoscope of emo-tions, many pleasurable. But He never intended for feelings to dominate our behavior. If our feel-ings governed us, we couldn't respond to prob-lems with a positive attitude, control our temper, harness our tongue, or live through temptations.

What would happen if, for one week, we

banned self-discipline and acted only on impulse? Think of the disastrous results on human relationships, business, peace negotiations, and waistlines! What if the Midas people didn't "feel" like installing your muffler? If your favorite disc jockey didn't "feel" like coming on the air? If the town's only heart specialist didn't "feel" like performing emergency surgery on your dad?

The test of a man or woman of God is how that person responds to the uninspired moment. Discipline is that quiet reserve that can help us pass the test.

Make self-discipline a life-style, not an isolated experience. James' ministry lasted about 30 years. That meant 10,957 days—including seven leap years—of plugging away for Jesus!

Christian maturity is a gradual process. It's a daily experience of getting to know Christ better and fulfilling His purposes in the world. Improving our self-mastery is part of the growing process. One dose of discipline isn't good for the long haul. The concentration we muster up during the week of final exams in May is good only for the demands of that week. Getting a fresh academic start in September calls for a fresh supply of discipline.

In 1972, I lost seventy pounds in four months. Keeping my weight normal requires regular, ongoing control of my eating.

Goals inspire us to execute self-discipline. To serve Christ was James' ambition. More specifically, he set goals of getting the young church in

Jerusalem organized and prodding Christians to apply their beliefs about Jesus to the nuts and bolts of life. As with James, setting goals can give us reasons to make the sacrifices demanded by discipline.

When Bart Conner was a 17-year-old high school senior from Skokie, Ill., he was the finest young gymnast in the United States. Bart won the state all-around championship as a sophomore, and in 1973, won the U.S. Gymnastics Federation's national Junior Olympics title. Bart's ultimate goal, is to win a medal in the 1980 Olympics.

In 1971, he began following a nine-year, highly disciplined developmental program. In an interview with a Chicago newspaper his senior year, Bart said, "Discipline is what makes great gymnasts—the time you spend in the gym, the patience you have, the dedication."

Bart's schedule in this nine-year program calls for six workouts a week, each from three to four hours long. "Sometimes I wonder if I can handle all the frustration and discipline," Bart admitted in the newspaper article. "Sure, there are times when I don't feel like going to the gym. But I want to be good, so I have to work. You see, I have a goal. And I must accept what I have to do to reach it."

What concrete goals could someone set who's trying to lose 15 pounds? get along with his friends and parents? get to know Jesus better?

Don't confuse legalism and self-discipline. A legalist is somebody who feels he "ought" to pray, to read the Bible, to witness. A legalist feels he has to perform certain duties in order to be acceptable to God. The legalist who has received Christ forgets that God accepts him just on the basis of Christ's merit, and that nothing he does or doesn't do can make him any more acceptable to God.

God wants Christians to pray, read the Bible, and witness. But He wants our behavior to be a loving response to a God who, because Jesus has paid the penalty for our sins, forgives us and loves us as we are. And love can be the reason for things we do whether or not our feelings cheer us on.

For instance, starting a quiet time of prayer and Bible reading can be motivated by legalism, and viewed as a burdensome regulation of a fun-hating God. Or it can be the fruit of self-discipline, viewed as something we need to survive as Christians in a non-Christian world. What's crucial is the motive behind the action.

Satan tries to confuse us. He suggests that if we don't really want to do something, we shouldn't do it. "You'll be a legalist and a hypocrite," he whispers. "God won't honor it if you aren't committed to it," he contends.

What is the flaw in Satan's argument? God measures commitment by *obedience*, not emotion! Perhaps the most imposing enemy of self-discipline is the rationalization, "That's too legalistic!" Even if we don't *feel* like opening our Bible, our motivation in doing so can still be right. It can be something I *will* to do, regardless of my feelings. It's *what* I do and *why* I do it that counts with God, not whether or not I have a natural inclination for it.

Think of James. He didn't keep the Nazarite vow or develop callouses on his knees in an effort to earn Brownie points with God. Instead, he knew that doing all those unpleasant things would help his relationship with God and his effectiveness as a church leader.

A college student I know wrestled with this problem. His strong desire to avoid hypocrisy and legalism kept him from regular Bible study. Then the Holy Spirit impressed him with the words found in James 1:25: "The man who looks into the perfect law, the law of liberty, and makes a habit of doing so, is not the man who hears and forgets. He puts that law into practice and he wins true happiness" (PH).

The student explained, "I didn't want my life to be governed by do's and don'ts, so to keep from being legalistic, I read the Bible only when the urge hit me. I figured I wouldn't get anything out of Bible study if I did it merely because I'm supposed to, or when I wanted to do something else.

"But this verse from James tells me to make a habit of Bible reading, regardless of what mood I'm in. My hang-up about being legalistic had been an excuse for my lack of diligence! It wasn't easy to follow James' advice, but I did improve my consistency. And a surprising thing happened. God began feeding me the most during the very sessions that I hadn't felt like starting.

Now I find myself *wanting* to have devotions more often."

Self-discipline is a by-product of a close relationship with Jesus. Often we look for help from Jesus, without seeking *Him.* We shoot quickie prayers to Jesus, asking for discipline, for patience, for this or that, without an earnest desire to know Him better. We want to use Him without confronting Him. We seek *something* from Him, but He doesn't give us something without giving us *Someone:* Himself!

Let's not put James on a pedestal. His self-mastery stemmed from a love and devotion to Jesus Christ. The power wasn't something he conjured up on his own. Trusting, not trying, made the difference in his life.

The Christian's inner reserve that makes self-control possible is the Holy Spirit, "who by His power within us is able to do immeasurably more than we ask or imagine" (Ephesians 3:20a, NIV). Self-control is a fruit of the Holy Spirit (Galatians 5:23). With God's provision, a disciplined person adequately rules himself. Every Christian has the same power source, the same capacity to practice self-control. But an inability to trust, inadequate knowledge of biblical teaching, and unconfessed sins can block the flow of God's power to a person. Undisciplined Christians aren't living in daily dependence on God's Spirit.

Ever heard of "The Rub Principle"? It claims that we become like the people we most often rub against. If we're around a grouchy boss eight hours a day, we tend to snap at other members of the family in the evening. If we stick close to a friend with a strong sense of humor, we start repeating his jokes and adopting some of his actions. Television programming research also supports this principle. Violent characters reproduce themselves in viewers.

That's the secret to improving our self-discipline—rubbing elbows with the most disciplined carpenter who ever lifted a hammer: Jesus Christ. If our first concern is knowing Him instead of using Him, benefits such as self-discipline become part of the package.

No one can package self-discipline separately, wrap it, and drop it in your lap as a birthday gift or Christmas present. There's no easy formula or pat answer on how to develop this quality. Whether or not you develop it depends, in part, on how you answer this question: Do I want to be an average, run-of-the-mill Christian, or do I want to be a disciple of Christ?

Etched on an old tombstone were these words: "Here lies a man who was going to . . . Now he's gone!" What's one thing you want to do that up till now, you've lacked the self-discipline to accomplish?

Mary of Bethany

8

The World's Largest Feet

On the West Coast of the United States, several people claim to have seen a gorilla-like monster. The reports say this beast has hair over its body like a monkey, but walks like a huge man. Some people have even claimed to have photographed the brute.

Even though the monster may well be nothing more than a joker in a monkey suit, it has gotten a name for itself. It's called "Big Foot" because of the huge size its paw prints are supposed to be.

But a person, who once walked this earth, probably had the world's largest feet—ever. And this person was no monster or ape-like creature. He was Jesus Christ. Throughout the Gospels, there are many times when people fell at Jesus' feet.

What value does a study of the people at Jesus' feet have for us today? How can first-century episodes in which people stayed at his feet help us deal with the problems we face at home, work, and school? Why did God inspire the human authors of the Bible to make so many references to this odd part of Jesus' body?

One Bible person we most often see at Jesus' feet is Mary, the sister of Martha and Lazarus. Let's look at what she was like and later see why she knelt at His feet.

Feet or Food?

Mary lived with her sister and brother in Bethany, a small village two miles southeast of Jerusalem. Jesus stayed in their home when He came to Jerusalem. Lazarus and his sisters were well-to-do and socially prominent, and often had guests in their home.

Luke describes the first New Testament episode that features Mary:

> As Jesus and the disciples continued on their way to Jerusalem they came to a village where a woman named Martha welcomed them into her home. Her sister Mary sat on the floor, listening to Jesus as He talked.

> But Martha was the jittery type, and was worrying over the big dinner she was preparing.

> She came to Jesus and said, "Sir, doesn't it seem unfair to You that my sister just sits here while I do all the work? Tell her to come and help me."

> But the Lord said to her, "Martha, dear friend, you are so upset over all these details! There is really only one thing worth being concerned about. Mary has discovered it—and I won't

take it away from her!" (Luke 10:38-42, LB).

In Palestine's dry climate, dust easily got on to the feet of travelers. Foot-washing was a customary way to greet guests. Mary probably washed Jesus' feet when He entered her house. Then she remained at His feet, captivated by Him. She forgot about helping Martha in the kitchen.

Jesus appreciated Martha's efforts. The reason she scurried around the kitchen was to make Jesus feel loved by providing a tasty meal. Her motive was good, but Jesus used the incident to teach about priorities. The good is often the enemy of the best! Even things that are good in themselves can crowd out our time alone with Jesus.

Jesus' Great Feat

Mary appears next in John 11, where the death and resurrection of her brother is described. Jesus, who was ministering in Perea, got word from Mary and Martha that Lazarus was sick. Rather than catching the next camel out of Perea, Jesus waited two days before leaving for Bethany. He allowed Lazarus to die.

Jesus' delay deeply hurt Mary. When she met Jesus on the outskirts of town, "She fell down at His feet, saying, 'Sir, if You had been here, my brother would still be alive'" (John 11:32, LB). Jesus promptly visited the tomb and raised her brother from death.

Mary and a large number of friends had been mourning inside her house. But the comfort of friends wasn't enough. She didn't run to Jesus expecting him to resurrect Lazarus. It helped just to drop her grief at His feet—before she knew He would reverse the tragedy. There was something about sharing her heartbreak with *Him* that made a difference.

There still is.

John describes a third time that Mary fell at Jesus' feet:

Six days before the Passover ceremonies began, Jesus arrived in Bethany where Lazarus was—the man he had brought back to life. A banquet was prepared in Jesus' honor. Martha served, and Lazarus sat at the table with Him. Then Mary took a jar of costly perfume made from essence of nard, and anointed Jesus' feet with it and wiped them with her hair. And the house was filled with fragrance.

But Judas Iscariot, one of His disciples—the one who would betray Him—said, "That perfume was worth a fortune. It should have been sold and the money given to the poor." Not that he cared for the poor, but he was in charge of the disciples' funds and often dipped into them for his own use!

Jesus replied, "Let her alone. She did it in preparation for My burial. You can always help the poor, but I won't be with you very long" (John 12:1-8, LB).

The perfume was worth a year's wages for an average worker. Mary figured that Jesus deserved the best.

What onlookers thought didn't matter to her. What Jesus thought did. A true worshiper never lets others dictate his response to Jesus.

Let's take a closer look at the three times Mary fell at Jesus' feet. What help do these episodes offer for people in a time preoccupied with Super Bowls and World Series?

Talk, Talk, Talk

Mary screened out the bustle around her and listened to what He said about God, man, current events, and the future.

There's talk today about dwindling food and energy supplies. But we'll never have to worry about a shortage of opinions. Newspaper and magazine editors reserve a page or more on which they print their perspectives on current events. Readers swamp publishers with letters in which they spout off on everything from the World Series to Supreme Court decisions. Whether we're talking about the front page, the Sports section, or the local TV news report, the going thing is to quote an "expert" or VIP.

On the basis of a person's fame, wealth, education, or position, we assign what is termed "credibility." It means we value what that person says and accept it as gospel.

But whatever happened to *God's* ideas? Even among Christians there's a scarcity of Bible reading, the most frequent way in which God speaks to us today.

In 1734 the military governor of Brandenburg, Germany died and his collection of books and manuscripts was auctioned. Among the things sold was a small bundle of handwritten music that brought only a small sum. The manuscripts passed from hand to hand till someone put them in the Berlin Royal Library. For more than a 100 years, the bundle of music remained unopened. The person who finally opened it found the original scores of Johann Sebastian Bach's six Brandenburg Concerti! Many had owned this treasure without bothering to look inside.

Almost everyone in the English-speaking world owns or has access to a Bible. But are we making regular withdrawals from this never-ending treasury of divine opinion? Mary had eyeball-to-eyeball contact with Jesus. She literally sat at His feet to hear Him. We "sit at Jesus' feet" for instruction when we "listen" to His written Word.

Listening to Jesus was more important to Mary than the meal Martha was fixing. I heard of a Christian leader who made a vow to God: "No Bible, no breakfast!" If he gets up late or some emergency gets in the way of his morning time at Jesus' feet, he also skips breakfast. "If I'm too busy to feed my soul," he says, "I'm too busy to feed my body."

A player for the San Diego Chargers made the same vow. For years he had disciplined his body, but he needed a little mental handle like this vow to achieve self-control in his devotional life.

Hundreds of years before Mary, Job also put the feast of God's words ahead of steak and eggs: "I have not refused His commandments but have enjoyed them more than my daily food" (Job 23:12, LB).

Is God a Crutch?

One of the greatest tests of Christian faith is how we react when something unpleasant happens. Adversity reveals the nuts and bolts of our faith. Why be a Christian if knowing Jesus can't make a difference in our responses to the ugly aspects of life? Crushed by Lazarus' death, Mary dropped her grief at Jesus' feet.

But not everyone leans on Jesus. An 18-year-old wrote a "last will and testament" following an argument with his girlfriend. Then he shot the 15-year-old girl twice and fatally wounded himself. Another young man was upset over a shattered romance. He also wounded his girlfriend and shot himself to death. These were extreme reactions. But the glut of violence, bitterness, and unhappiness in our world shows that people aren't standing in line to fall at Jesus' feet.

Both the Old and New Testaments stress that a burden can't be on our shoulders and at His feet at the same time: "Give your burdens to the Lord. He will carry them" (Psalm 55:22, LB). "Let Him have all your worries and cares, for He is always thinking about you and watching everything that concerns you" (1 Peter 5:7, LB).

When a man I know was in high school, an accident killed his 15-year-old sister. A few hours later, his mom led the family in a study of God's love and faithfulness from Romans 8. Their time of study and prayer "at Jesus' feet" didn't instantly erase their pain. But 30 years later, the girl's brother vividly remembers the supernatural support found that evening.

When we put burdens at Jesus' feet, as Mary put her burden of grief there, He sometimes uses His power to reverse the negative circumstances. But more often, He reverses our inner state. He enables us to respond to tragedy supernaturally instead of naturally. He turns anxiety into peace and self-reliance into a humble dependence on Him. He's more interested in changing people than things. Troubles are one means by which He achieves positive change in us.

Some people mock the habit of going to Jesus with problems. During a Sunday night rap session between a pastor and a group of students, a girl blurted out, "I can't stand this a minute longer! God's nothing but a crutch. He's a figment of the imagination of weak people. He's a product of your own inadequacy."

Here's how the pastor responded:

"Imagine you have a skiing accident and you're taken to the hospital. They put your leg in a plaster cast and give you a piece of wood with a rubber ring on one end, a pad on the other end, and a handle half way down it. I can just see you now—you grab that piece of wood and rap the doctor over the head with it. After you beat him to a pulp, you scream 'It's a crutch! I hate crutches!'

"Of course, you wouldn't do that at all. Because when you have a broken leg, you're thankful for the support of crutches. I admit, without apology, that God is my crutch. I have a broken leg, spiritually speaking. And if it weren't for the growing relationship I have with Jesus, I'd be limping along worse than I am. This doesn't mean I invented God. I've merely learned that I can't cope without leaning on Him. He's the only One who is adequate for my inadequacy."

Mary reminds us that it's OK to cry for help. That's what Jesus is for.

God Makes House Calls

Rubbing Jesus' feet with costly perfume was Mary's way of worshiping Jesus. Put simply, worship is mental and emotional preoccupation with God. Worship can occur at any place and time, so long as the Lord is the object.

I call my most unforgettable worship experiences my "burning bushes." A "burning bush" is any place where I've enjoyed a close encounter with God. The Old Testament book of Exodus tells how God spoke to Moses out of a burning bush in the wilderness. I can meet God anywhere. He isn't confined to Sunday morning and Wednesday evening office hours at a local church. Any place can become a sacred shrine from which God speaks to me, or at which something happens to make me appreciate who He is or something He's done.

My "burning bushes" have included the driver's seat of a car, a pitcher's mound at midnight, and the floor of a walk-in closet. I remember life-changing moments of prayer in these places. Your burning bushes may be a lounge chair in the school library or your bed, as you peer out the window at the majesty of the Milky Way and Big Dipper. You may find God in biology lab, where the intricacies of creation re-

veal His genius. He may be in the family room of
a home as friends share how God has been working in their lives, or in the shower, where you
serenade Him with choruses. With God, any old
bush will do! Like Mary, we worship at His feet
anytime we give Him undivided, affectionate
attention.

Worship is for the *Lord's* benefit as well as
ours. Jesus showed the importance of Mary's devotion. Think of it: The Creator of the universe
enjoys spending time alone with me! "I want you
to realize that God has been made rich because
we who are Christ's have been given to Him!"
(Ephesians 1:18, LB).

Room for More

Besides their atheistic bent, what do Nazi chief
Adolf Hitler, former Soviet head Joseph Stalin,
and feisty, Bible-berating Madalyn Murray
O'Hair have in common?

Like Mary, they'll someday fall at Jesus' feet!
Everyone will one day acknowledge that He is
the Son of God, even those with an atheistic bent:
"At the name of Jesus every knee shall bow in
heaven and on earth and under the earth, and
every tongue shall confess that Jesus Christ is
Lord, to the glory of God the Father"
(Philippians 2:10-11, LB).

For many, that admission will come too late.

Why can we say Jesus has the world's largest
feet? Because no matter how many needs we
drop at His feet, or how many of us fall at His
feet, there's always room for more!

Stephen

9

Being a Winner

In sports, what counts most is winning. Coming out on top. Few people brag about a second-place trophy. We've all heard the phrase, "It's not whether you win or lose, but how you play the game." But a famous athlete said, "You won't find that posted in a *winner's* locker room!"

Most sports award their winners with a visual symbol that identifies them as victors. Bruce Jenner, decathlon champion in the 1976 Olympics at Montreal, got a gold medal placed around his neck. Members of the National Football League championship team get "Super Bowl" rings. The 25 baseball players who brave the October chill and win wear World Series rings.

My great moment in sports came when I accepted a Southeastern Regional Championship trophy for our Teener baseball team. Before the big game, I watched a tournament official lug the trophy to the press box. Throughout the game, when I'd let a guy get on base I'd remember that trophy. It inspired my best pitching effort.

They didn't have Howard Cosell to ask them stupid questions, $3 million contracts, or Aqua-Velva commercials to film on their days off, but athletes were important in the first century too. Cities such as Corinth annually staged sports events, including boxing and foot races. After each contest, the victor got a crown or wreath to adorn his head. The Greek word for this victor's crown was "stephanos." Spectators readily identified as winners those participants donning a "stephanos."

From the word "stephanos," we derive the name "Stephen." The biblical character Stephen, described in Acts 6 and 7, was appropriately named. In God's eyes, he won in life. He was a spiritual champion. In tough situations, he successfully reflected Christlike character. He was a model of the type of service God rewards.

What does it take to live life to the fullest—without latching on to worldly gusto? Is the world right when it promotes luck, good looks, muscle, money, and brains as the answers? What is the key to strong Christian character and usefulness to God's kingdom? A close look at Stephen's life answers these questions. Let's look at some of Stephen's characteristics and see how they came about.

Gusto Living

Stephen lived a "full" life. Because he was "full of the Spirit and of wisdom" as well as faith

(Acts 6:3, 5, NASB), first-century believers selected him to head up a food program for widows. His being "full of grace and power" (6:8) explains how he performed miracles among the people. Unbelievers unjustly stoned him to death (Acts 7:55-60). But his short life shows us the power God makes available to every Christian.

Today's exploding statistics on suicide indicate that many people do not live a "full" life. In the United States, suicide is the second leading cause of death among young people. Suicide kills more Canadians between ages 15 and 30 than any other cause but one. Every year, 25 to 30 students from each of Toronto's major high schools attempt to kill themselves.

In just five days in 1977, 132 calls poured in to one city's suicide prevention hotline. Many who called brought up actor Freddie Prinze's suicide earlier that year. (Prinze was star of TV's *Chico and the Man*.) A coordinator for this telephone service commented, "They talked of how Prinze had chosen to end his life when he had everything to live for, so why should they continue when they had very little to live for?"

If you think the Christian life is trouble-free, you're kidding yourself. But a Christian who relies on a relationship with Christ rather than on things around him can be content. Was Jesus only kidding when He said, "My purpose is to give life in all its fullness"? (John 10:10, LB)

Humility marked Stephen's attitude. To let the Twelve Apostles spend more time studying and praying, Stephen willingly served widows. He didn't feel low just because his job wasn't as glamorous as the others'. No competitive spirit thwarted his effectiveness. God later rewarded his obedience to a "lower class" job by giving him an important role in evangelism.

Years ago, a friend of mine got a position as a magazine editor. At the time I was between jobs and uncertain about my future. I knew God had plans for me that didn't include a career in journalism. But I was jealous. I figured I was just as qualified as my friend for that magazine position. "Why didn't they interview *me*?" I pouted. I realize now that my jealousy was pride breaking out all over me.

How you *react* to situations exposes the depth of your Christian faith. What do you think about a teammate who starts the game while you sit on the bench? Or about the popular girl who won the last cheerleading spot which you dreamed about? About the older brother or sister who gets better grades than you do?

Stephen got the message across about the good news of Christ. Skeptical opponents of Christianity didn't know how to deal with Stephen's sensible and enthusiastic preaching (Acts 6:10). Their response to Stephen's message revealed the impact of his words: "when they heard this, they were cut to the quick" (7:54, NASB). His success didn't come from his smooth-talking way, but from a reliance on God's Spirit and a real knowledge of the Bible.

What reasons do people give for not becoming Christians?

"Christianity is boring."

"Christianity is too confining."

"I'm just not the religious type."

"*All* religions lead to God."

"It doesn't matter what you believe, so long as you're sincere."

"I'm not good enough to be a Christian. My past is terrible."

"Jesus was just a good man, a great moral teacher."

"There are too many hypocrites in the church."

How would you answer each objection? What Bible truths could you use to handle each one? Are you ready "to make a defense to everyone who asks you to give an account for the hope that is in you"? (1 Peter 3:15, NASB)

God doesn't give everyone his own microphone to broadcast His message. But He does give every Christian opportunities to share the Word with others.

Stephen had a good reputation. Church leaders trusted him enough to have him work for them. But even members of the Jewish Council, who were trying him on false charges, "saw his face like the face on an angel" (6:15, NASB). They couldn't banish his radiance or extinguish his composure.

The Bible says, "A good name is more to be desired than great riches; favor is better than silver or gold" (Proverbs 22:1, NASB). Perhaps the highest praise that can be given to a Christian is for someone to point to him and say, "That guy's for real!"

During rough times, Stephen concentrated on Jesus Christ. As his enemies prepared to stone him, Stephen "gazed intently into heaven and saw the glory of God, and Jesus standing at the right hand of God" (Acts 7:55, NASB). When things look tough, we usually pity ourselves and whine. But Stephen shows how our trust in Christ can supernaturally change our responses to problems. The security of our relationship with Him goes beyond circumstances.

After I finished school, I wanted one job, but another person was picked instead. I remember slumping on a park bench and crying. I pitied myself for losing that opportunity. Only when my thoughts turned away from the job and toward Jesus, did my peace return. My prayer changed from "Why, Lord?" to "What else do You have in store for me?" As my outlook on the situation changed, so did my feelings.

Stephen forgave those who hurt him. Jewish authorities secretly bribed men to speak out against him in public. Then when they arrested Stephen and charged him with perverting their beliefs about God and the Law, they also brought to the trial witnesses they'd coaxed into lying. But Stephen asked the Lord not to hold his killers' sin against them (Acts 7:60).

A more common response to being wronged is bitterness.

One morning an 11-year-old boy was awakened by the sound of a gunshot. He rushed downstairs and saw his mother lying on the floor, blood gushing from a gunshot wound in her head.

His father, with a gun in hand, lay near her, seriously wounded.

The boy rushed to a phone and called an ambulance. His father lay between life and death for several days, but finally recovered—though he was partially paralyzed. Throughout the father's time in the hospital, his son stayed away.

"It was just so horrible," the son recalled a few years later. "I just couldn't forgive him for what he did to Mom."

But God led the son away from his bitterness. "I was reading the Bible one night," he said, "when I came across a passage that hit right home. I realized I hadn't been the forgiving person that God wanted me to be."

The boy had come across this passage from Hebrews 12:15: "Look after each other so that not one of you will fail to find God's best blessings. Watch out that no bitterness takes root among you, for as it springs up it causes deep trouble, hurting many in their spiritual lives" (LB).

In spite of Stephen's sins, he knew Christ had forgiven him. Perhaps that explains how he so readily forgave his enemies. No matter how others hurt us, we're responsible for how we respond to them.

Formula for Victory

What was responsible for Stephen's strong faith? His power over satanic forces? His sensitivity to the Holy Spirit? What made him effective in sharing his faith and answering the objections of unbelievers? What gave him the strength to calmly be personally wronged and to forgive his enemies?

It wasn't that he had a higher IQ or that he was a Robert Redford look-alike that made Stephen a winner. He wasn't a supersaint in whom God created an extra gland that secreted spirituality. Like us, he probably moaned through tooth decay and overslept on the day of an important event.

What made Stephen a winner was his intense love for the Word of God. His defense before the Jewish authorities revealed a deep knowledge of the Old Testament. Without prepared notes or cue cards, he quoted accurately from Old Testament books.

A young evangelist asked hundreds of Christian young people if they had a daily devotional time. Can you guess the response? *Only 3% said they did!* Most young Christians consider their devotional lives a disaster area; yet many of them wonder why they have spiritual problems.

Why is spiritual starvation such a big problem? Satan fights to keep us away from God's Word. Other things always seem more pressing. It's hard to make the quiet time meaningful, so we get discouraged. We miss once, and it keeps happening. We know we *should* study the Bible, yet we subconciously wonder what difference it makes in the nitty-gritty of school, work, and family situations.

Ty Gable of Jackson, Miss. became more consistent in his devotions after he discovered a need to memorize Scripture. "There's just one bad thing about the Bible," he said. "It's almost never with me when I need it the most! Back in high school there was this one guy who really irritated me. He could get under my skin for no good reason, and a lot of times I felt like telling him to hang it. I was sure the Bible would have something to help me at a time like that, but the Bible wasn't around."

Ty started memorizing Scripture so he'd have it when he needed it. Before long, meeting his "friend" in the hall, chunks of 1 Corinthians 13 would pop into his mind: "Love is patient, love is kind . . . not arrogant." The power of the Bible kept him from a major blowup. Ty says his memory work "gives the Holy Spirit something to work with at the times when I really need it."

Promises, Promises

The Bible gives two promises of success. In each case, the formula is the same. God said to Joshua that if he would meditate in the Scriptures, "then [he would] make [his] way prosperous, and then [he would] have success" (Joshua 1:8, NASB). Also, someone who concentrates on God's Word:

Will be like a tree firmly planted by streams of water,

Which yields its fruit in its season,

And its leaf does not wither;

And in whatever he does, he prospers (Psalm 1:3, NASB).

Following in Stephen's footsteps is possible because his steps were directed by God's Word. In fact, we have access to a resource unavailable to Stephen—the New Testament.

Even in death, Stephen proved a winner. His courageous stand for Christ led other members of the early church to preach boldly despite the threat of death. Instead of putting out the flame of the Gospel, persecutions that followed the stoning of Stephen merely fanned it. And his forgiving spirit while being stoned impressed a man named Saul, who witnessed and approved the execution. That Pharisee, also known as Paul, later received Christ and became a founder of many first-century churches.

I named my second child "Stephen." I want him to love and to use God's Word as did this Bible personality. What the Bible did for Stephen, it can do for my son.

And for you.

MORE GREAT BOOKS FROM SONPOWER